Jacoby

Where Galaxies Kiss the Earth

Ethers of Eternal Bloom

Written by: Jesse J. Jacoby

Soulspire Publishing
Truckee, Ca, 96161

ISBN: 979-8-9900273-4-3
Library of Congress Control Number: 2012921011

Cover art, font, and layout are all original art by Gabriela Mejia

Dedication

This book is dedicated to the Feminine Divine – she represents the keeper of wisdom, vessel of creation, and rhythm of the unseen.

Her intuition is an unshaken current, flowing through time with quiet knowing.

Her goodness is impenetrable, a force that neither storm nor shadow can undo.

Her butterfly wings flutter forever, even if she insists for only a day.

The good and wild in her are equally lovely, for she was never meant to be tamed.

Everyone who encounters her walks away enlivened, enriched – marked by the essence of something sacred.

Her pollen has sent treasure hunters on endless quests, searching for the source of her light.

She is confident and secure, yet boundlessly free.

She is giving and pure yet never emptied.

She is the pulse of love, the quiet architect of healing.

Her heart holds earthly cures and whispered remedies from stars.

A sacred presence, both tender and unyielding.

Jacoby

Invocation of the Muse

The more we open our hearts to love, the greater our chances of being visited by a muse – those ethereal whispers of inspiration that dance between worlds.

These sprite spirits are drawn to authenticity, ignited by passion, and enchanted by raw creativity. They do not dwell where falseness lingers; they seek the luminescent souls who dare to embody truth.

When we become mindful of the energies we attract and expend, we do more than summon muses – we manifest them, braiding them into the currents of our life force.

Sincerity vibrates at the pinnacle of existence.

Genuineness sings in the realm of the divine,
a purity so radiant even the unseen gathers near.

Realness carries a grace so undisturbed, the invisible drifts closer.

A brilliance so true, the immaterial listens.

Map of Luminous Verses

Jacoby

The Unbroken Wheel: A Love That Knows No Bounds

"Angry people want you to see how powerful they are. Loving people want you to know how powerful you are." — Chief Red Eagle

Love is the most spoken yet least understood language of humankind. Whether we invoke in prayers, inscribe in poetry, or wear as a badge of virtue, how often do we truly embody her essence? With what cadence do we weave tenderness, devotion, and reverence into the fabric of our being, not just for those who reflect our own light, but for all things, even those cast in shadow?

We speak of love as something we give and receive, a transaction of sentiment, a measure of worthiness. Love, however, in true form, is unbound. This is a force that moves rivers to carve canyons, compels the sun to kiss the earth each morning, drives the unseen roots of trees to intertwine beneath soil, strengthening one another without expectation. Love is a frequency, a force, a current that flows through all things – whether we choose to align with or elude her magnitude.

For how many dawns have we let the tides of hostility and judgment erode the softness of our hearts? In a world of fragmented wishes and unfulfilled promises, how do we attune ourselves to the radiant vibration of pure adoration? Can we truly dismantle war with instruments of peace? Can we stand as unwavering sentinels of love, even when faced with cruelty?

Nature offers us a profound truth: love is not selective. A flower does not choose who may inhale her fragrance; she offers her scent freely, even to the hands that crush her petals. The sun does not withhold warmth from those who have turned away from light. Trees extend their shade to all, even a logger who comes with an axe. Bees pollinate our fields despite the toxins we have exposed them to.

This love, given without condition, without exception, is the highest form of grace. For this is the love of the cosmos, the love of creation herself.

To cast aside those who walk in wickedness may appear easy. To deem them undeserving of our compassion is executed rhythmically with no questions of morale. Love that is conditional though is not love at all. This is convenience – a fleeting favor.

To love only when easy is to deny love's true nature. When we sever our devotion for one, we risk fraying the entire fabric of our ability to love at all. Love is a revolution of the soul, a radical act of choosing connection where separation seeks to thrive. To ride the wheel of love is to abandon the illusion of division and to embrace unity as an immutable truth.

When love becomes the foundation of our being, we no longer reduce force to mere words. *I love you* is no match for the felt experience of oneness – the deep, visceral recognition of another's pain as our own, of their joy as an extension of our heartbeat.

True love is not performative. This is a reverence for all things. An unshakable allegiance to harmony, a commitment to see and honor the sacred in all beings – whether human, animal, insect, tree, stone, soil, sky, or alien.

Scattered among the joys and triumphs of existence are echoes of a world in peril. There are those who live with their eyes closed, unaware of the suffering that unfolds in silent corners – genocide, exploitation, war, and wounds left festering in the absence of love. These wounds will not be healed by condemnation or vengeance; they will only be healed by the highest form of love – one that does not waver, does not bargain, and does not need validation.

Osho reminds us: *"To flow and grow in love needs no perfection. Love has nothing to do with the other. A loving person simply loves, just as an alive person breathes, drinks, eats, and sleeps."* Love is not something we strive for but something we become. When we extend grace without effort, when we uplift others as naturally as we exhale, we will begin to understand his depths.

This collection of writings is a testament to love's infinite nature, an invitation to recognize that love is not something scarce, fragile, or transactional, but an entity that is abundant, eternal, and ever turning, like the great wheel of life. We refer to a force that, once aligned with, can never be broken.

Take this journey with me. Step into a world where disparity dissolves, where light emanates from every crevice and atom, where love is no longer a fleeting ideal but the very breath of existence.

"You must love in such a way that the world you love is free." — Thich Nhat Hanh

Nebula I: Celestial Invitations

Love, in true form, is written in stars – a cosmic whisper, a gravitational pull, an infinite unfolding of devotion.

Before two souls intertwine, before destiny unveils itself, there is an invitation – an awakening, a beckoning, a call from the heavens.

This section is a journey into the threshold of sacred love, where mystery meets magnetism, where longing meets the celestial unknown.

These poems are stardust in motion, constellations forming, the first breath of something eternal.

Love is not merely discovered. We remember.

The cosmic force has always existed, waiting for us to recognize our reflection in another.

These verses speak to the pull of kindred spirits, the silent knowing in a gaze, the moment two energies collide and the universe expands to make room for their merging.

Here, the galaxies align, the veil lifts, and the cosmos extends a hand.

Step forward.

Love is calling.

The Sixth Element

I look into her eyes and whisper stories
of how indecision has died.

Darkness is always drawn to light, and I have met
an essence that illuminates the abyss of night with
her morning star shine.

I held her in my arms and felt all doubt dissolve –
a certainty so absolute, even the echoes of past lives
could not erase the realness.

These feelings will never evanesce.

I traveled back in time and saw her painted in
hieroglyphs, etched on cave walls, her image
transcending centuries.

I rummaged through the annals of ancient cultures who once worshipped her grace with a reverence akin to my own – a devotion to being a loyal man.

There is safety and security woven into the rhythm of her breath.

We are a vibe, one we feel more than we see.

The hues of redwood bark and rainbow eucalyptus trees blend in the palette of her spirit.

Her beauty seized my frequency, a glow so golden, even the moon envies her radiance.

Night stars dance in her galaxy.
Celestial queens marvel at her potency.
She is the empress of violet flame.

Uncertainty is instantly slain, and my heart – officially claimed.

Her iris holds tanzanite shades, her character forged from jadeite.

Yet no gem in this world outshines her richness of spirit.

The brightness she emits is atavistic, a beacon passed through generations.

Mystics spend lifetimes seeking unity with the deity – the very embodiment of who she is.

She is the Sixth Element, the fifth direction on my medicine wheel.

In her presence, duality dissolves, for there is no polarity to divinity.

Everything about her is real.

I would spend eternity unearthing the mystery of her intricacy, learning the language of her being, deciphering the scriptures written in the light of her gaze.

As Oshun's mirror reflects once more from her gleam, the last of humanity's sorrows fall free – flowing with the rivers, merging into the vastness of the sea.

If I Were the Moon

Your glow is an ember from Source, an emblem of life force, a pulse of radiance that ripples wherever you are.

If I were the moon, I would hold all your secrets in my glow, wrap them in silver hush, never let them go.

I would watch in quiet admiration as the rose garden of your soul blooms, petals unfolding like whispered prayers to the infinite sky.

Your light is a beacon for all, a guiding star for wandering hearts, a lotus in the midday sun, whose florets make the sun pause to dance.

You are more than bright – you are brilliance herself.

A channel of wisdom from ancient times, a living scripture, a portal to Christ.

Your aura is the color of fauna and flora, of mist rising from waterfalls, of dusk as she kisses dawn.

You are the wind moving tides, the fire that warms earth, rain that washes away what is heavy, and the breath between creation.

We are drawn together by the unseen forces that compose us – light, love, and eternity woven into form.

Altar of Wild Suns

I lay you upon the altar of wild suns, where
untamed love burns like celestial fire and blossoms
in the cradle of nature's endless exhale.

We are a constellation of fingertips and whispers,
a solar storm of passion and gravity, dancing inside
the anatomy of a universe that pulses as intimately
as our own skin.

Distance distorts into devotion, folding into the
fabric of time, where light bends, and longing
dissolves into the colors of an aurora only we have
the eyes to see.

Kaleidoscopic hues spill from the seams of our
being, weaving every moment between us into a
tapestry of fire-lit wonder.

We cherish the filaments of what remains – from
the first kiss to the finality of our fusion, from the
embered sighs to the cosmic crescendo of a love
that has never known extinction.

You are a cell in the body of the universe.

I shoot star-shells of wisdom straight into the
depths of your spirit, so that in the bursting light,
you may see for yourself the truth of what I have
always known.

You are a citizen of the cosmos, a melody
composed of solar flares and lunar hymns.

Every inhale, a sacred chant to the universe, the air you draw, a silent prayer to the constellations.

Your exhale dissolves into the music of the cosmos.

And I am a privileged, one-member audience, in awe of how lyrical your existence is.

Keeper of the Nebulae

You are made of water that hydrates souls for eternity with only one sip.

A single drop of you is enough to quench lifetimes.

Your spirit has been dancing longer than fungi have woven mycelium threads beneath ancient forests, dating further back than spores have drifted through the wind, seeding life into the soil.

When you laugh, the microorganisms that stitch this planet together smile wider than all four oceans combined.

Your smile is a constellation, a celestial map guiding unseen travelers – an alien species peering through distant lenses witnessing the miracle of your light.

Your eyes are waterfalls, cascading from undiscovered mountains hidden in the sky's embrace, flowing with the wisdom of places even the stars have yet to explore.

Your voice ripples through time, sending waves into the future, a frequency so pure even the sun pauses to listen.

You are the whisper of every sunrise, the hush between each heartbeat.

When I look at you, I see the purest love – untouched by time, unburdened by sorrow.

A love that creates worlds simply by existing.

Objet d'Art

An objet d'art – a creation of undeniable worth,
a masterpiece sculpted by unseen hands.

When I first saw her, my rhodopsin receptors
flared awake, an immediate response to the
magnitude of her allure.

The "disco ball effect" is an unworthy metaphor –
no, her iridescence did not merely shimmer;
she burnished the very atmosphere, imbuing the
space with a light that belonged only to her.

She was the focal point, the salience of elegance.
Mouths parted. Heads turned.

An unspoken hush fell in reverence.

Her essence – potent piquancy, a spice the tongue
cannot name, yet craves all the same.

My optic nerve developed a singular appetite,
fixated on the depth of her irises cerulean hues –
a blue so distinct, so uncharted, she infused my
world with pigments unknown to my soul.

Then, came the warning:

"Be careful."
"Wait until you see her true colors."

But what does that even mean?
Authenticity is the only luxury I desire.

Who settles for a lab-grown diamond when the fire of a natural stone sings history in light?

Cubic zirconia could never rival the depths of the real thing.

I seek sapphire, not spinel.
I attract pearls, not their synthetic ghosts.

These imitations, these polished veneers, are nothing but reflections of personas – masks cast over the truth of who someone really is.

And what if her 'true colors' are triadic –
bold, clashing, alive?

What if they are dark and tantric, or a fusion of tragic and romantic?

She carries the pigments of a Gouldian finch, a brushstroke of calcarifera ordinata, a prismatic spectrum, like the celestial space above a mandrill's lips.

Her complexion glows with the mystery of a mandarinfish, an impossible collision of hues.

Her kaleidoscopic smile – as hypnotic as a scarlet macaw's plumage, painting the air with brilliance.

Even in contrast, when she waltzes with darkness, or stumbles in shadow, she holds the majesty of a white tigress, grace in every measured step.

Have you ever held obsidian, watched a hidden fire tremble beneath crust, a glow waiting to break free?

Labradorite, unpolished, still breathes radiance.

A raven in flight, black feathers gilded by twilight's touch.

A melanistic jaguar, unseen yet undefeated, with rosettes defiant against the jungle's veil.

And her presence – without adornment, without embellishment, in baggy sweats or in silk, supersedes the need for anything meretricious.

She is the full spectrum, a frequency that bends and refracts, wavelengths of mystery and magnetism.

I marvel at the totality of her light.

I rank the eminence of what our connection means to me.

Golden Ratio

Fibonacci spirals woven in disc florets of sunflowers replicate the curls of your hair. Every strand – a golden ratio.

Corona filaments of blue passion flowers have glints of your iris. Your eyes are channels to Isis. I see oceans and tropical isles.

The way your teeth sparkle reminds me of the ice caves in Mendenhall glacier. Sirius shines all day through your smile.

Ancient light reflects from your clavicle line like bioluminescent waves brighten River Derwent in Tasmania.

I "feel" colors when I connect with you. They are born from the same earth tones as redwood bark and Rainbow Mountain in Peru.

Somewhere off the African coast, on the island of Mauritius, there are eccentric sand dunes immune to erosion known as Seven Colored Earths. Terres de Sept couleurs. They almost match your aesthetic allure.

On the floor of the River of Five Colors in Colombia, a plant species emits a pinkish hue that emanates through the surface of the water.

The macarenia clavigera.
This luster is reminiscent of your lips.

Your strength, the magnitude of tungsten.

Your voice, a human version of the chorus of katydids.

Your laugh, the song of the whippoorwill.

Your frequency is immeasurable.
The supremacy of your beauty is not contestable.

A Wish That Mended Time

One day, I found a genie's lamp, with a glow humming ancient promise.

Only one wish could be granted.

I asked to lift the weight from your spirit, to unshackle you from sorrow's grasp.

She agreed – on one condition: that my pain, too, would dissolve into stardust.

With a breath as soft as moonlight, she revived your confidence, stitched vitality back into your bones.

Your innocence, once fractured, is now restored.

She gave back the strength in your voice before the world could steal your confidence and walked back the shadows that trailed your past.

She freed you from the cruelty of this world, reminded you how to smile – not for survival, but as universal truth.

She turned time in her palm, offering you a return – to the moment before sorrow was etched in your skin.

With wisdom as your shield, you would never carve the same wound twice.

Then she paused, eyes reflecting wonder.

For even without tragedy's weight, before the storms – you were already radiant.

She saw you unchanged, unshaken, a beauty untouched by time.

A simple reminder:

Your light has never been replaceable.

The Woman Who Makes Wolves Swoon

"There are all kinds of love in this world, but never the same love twice."

She moves like freedom – ripened by time,
unshaken by storms, sweetness distilled from
Eden's orchards.

I watch in awe as she unfurls, a woman aching to
exhume herself from a shell that could never
contain her vastness.

She repels timidity, and we hear the knell of a girl
who once swallowed her voice now singing
farewell.

Governed only by moon cycles, she makes Artemis
proud.

Momus bows to her realness.

She has rewritten the code, broken the glitch,
even Athena steps aside in quiet reverence.

She teaches me to see the oceans for what they are –
not just water, but memory, rhythm, breath.
Each wave, each ripple, a reflection of her heart.
Yemaya cradles her in strong arms.

I take a step back as she makes art with her
movement, spinning honey from roses and
sorrows, a sacred alchemy only she understands.
She decorates sunsets with the colors of her smile,
leaving the sky breathless in her wake.

A different kind of apparatus, there is no denying the impression she leaves on nature's canvas.

A woman with a good heart and a wild soul, she jives to Earth's rhythms, entrancingly careening her hips beneath the moon's glow.

The kind of woman who makes wolves swoon.

Sensitivity flowers across her luminous cheeks, her graceful tears exudate – watering the soil with what no longer serves her on the way.

A mystery more affluent than the shores of Socotra, a direct descendant of Ra, her song is not of mediocrity, but of excellence and supremacy.

And as she writes her chapters, may I be her ink, the sustenance that keeps her story going?

Let her use me for all her guilty pleasures – for the depth of my love for her is beyond measure.

That Look You Give Me

I would hold you for a million years, my arms an eternal refuge, a sanctuary where time dissolves and love remains.

My shoulder will dry a galaxy of your tears, turning sorrow into stardust, letting the night sky wear your pain like a constellation of resilience.

I will love you for a thousand lifetimes, revive you whenever you die, breathe you back into existence with whispers of devotion stronger than time.

Love is more than all the riches a man could offer.

Love is the center of everything, the fabric of the unseen, the rhythm that keeps creation spinning.

Love is that look you give me, the unspoken promise, the missing piece that vanishes when you are gone.

I will be here when you are feeling low, laughing with you when you are alone, standing by your side forever.

Love is more than we can see, but I see you in everything.

Your smile could make me happy for a million years.

I could drown in your eyes for a thousand lifetimes and wish not to come up for air.

I would hold you for a million years.

I will love you for a thousand lifetimes.

Because love is that look you give me, the piece of me that is always missing when you are gone.

Deity in Flesh

I see you as a deity, a divine descent from indigenous royalty, the embodiment of every goddess – reincarnated into delicate flesh and tenderness.

Your goodness is incorruptible, your discipline, impenetrable.

Da Vinci would have forsaken Mona Lisa to immortalize the traces of your radiance, to capture the light that spills from your skin, the face that will leave a mark upon the soul of humankind.

Your smile awakens a longing in me – a hunger for devotion, for the deepest loyalty.

The portals in your eyes pull me home, back to my center, guiding me toward the man I was always meant to be.

You shape me into the ruler destiny demands, whisper secrets of true kingship into my soul, remind me that a leader's power is in his heart, not his throne.

You reveal to me the actual weight of a crown, Reminding me the meaning of being a King.

Not through command, but through the subtle ways you carry your dignity, preserve your sanctity, move through this world with unshaken grace.

Your womb is a pristine temple, a vessel of life force that no scale could ever measure.

Every particulate of your essence is sacred.

If I could trace the source of your sustenance, I would drink deep from the well, grow in gratitude, and awaken dormant wisdom that has slept within my lineage for generations before me.

You hold the power to command oceans, and my energy waves rise in reverence to meet you.

You are the one who makes Satan surrender to God.

Mistress of the elementals – when you speak, I feel them shift the space around me.

I can taste your brilliance in the cadence of your words, the way you sculpt meaning from syllables and silence.

You are the foundation of my adoration.

I stand heart wide open, manifesting, praying – that I may be chosen to embrace the full potency of your *activation.*

Immeasurable

Our first kiss taught my lips the language of satiety – a sensation so vast, so immeasurable, that hunger ceased to exist.

Her saliva – the most delicate edible, a sacred element, potent enough to transmute a predatory demon into embracing celibacy.

Her eyes blind me to adultery and unveil the vision of oneness.

Through them, I touch eternity.

I inhale the essence of her pheromones, filling my chest with the breath of the Most High.

Her wholeness regenerates my lungs, purifies the spaces that once held impurity.

My lymphatic fluid parts ways with promiscuity.

My cells bathe in an empowering substance, something my body has never known before.

I hold her hand, and in this touch – devotion is captured.

She is a mermaid who has swam the deepest oceans.

A supernova in the shadow of dawn.
A luminous God-star veiling the sun.
A radiant titan of the heavens.
A cosmic beacon beyond daylight's reach.

In the realm of thin air and silent gods, I witness her divine fire.

Her radiance crowns the summit of the highest peaks.

She is the apical meristem in the roots that hold me together.

She makes the man in me better.

A Mark Beyond Flesh

My mind keeps flashing the looks I cannot escape.

A monsoon could not wash them away, an imprint so profound not even vinyl could erase.

They are etched into my memory – permanent as constellations in a midnight sky.

I know who they belong to.

Maybe I am crazy, but I am not a fool.

If I were botanical ink, your whole body would be my tattoo.

Every inch of you, a canvas, every breath, a stroke of devotion.

Your sleeves would be a lioness – fierce, untamed, protector of realms.

Your poetry would fill the rest, flowing through your veins like scripture written in moonlight.

Your ribs would hold verses whispered between celestial bodies, your spine traced with mantras that only silence understands.

I would shade your clavicle with the echoes of our past lives, outline your hips with golden hymns only the wind remembers.

No needle needed, just the permanence of my reverence – a love so indelible that will not fade, or wane, or run.

Because you are already inked into me.

Gaia In You

Roll around in the mud.

Stain your skin in all of Earth's colors.

Let her dry on you like a prayer, as the sun bakes her into your being.

Lips like perfect rose petals, soft as morning's first blush.

Eyes like rivers, flowing pure, reflecting depths of things that cannot be spoken.

Your smile blooms flowers from cracked pavement, roots breaking through stone just to reach you – to bask in your light.

Climbing out, stretching high, even Haleakalā sunsets bow to the way you paint the sky.

Plants compose symphonies in rhythm with your vibrations, each leaf singing in tune with the pulse of your breath.

Speak – and Gaia whispers with you, your voice an echo of hers.

Your happiness paints rainbow eucalyptus trees, brushstrokes of joy dripping onto bark.

Stars dance naked in twilight, swaying to your presence, morning and night.

The makeup you wear was applied at birth – raw, radiant, divine.

I watch you serenade the sky, a hymn only nature understands.

You Are a Goddess

I want to read poetry that constructs the complexities of you – to decipher the verses woven into the fabric of your mind, where every stanza shines with the beauty of your soul.

I could listen to the expressive, rhythmic literary work of your imagination for a thousand lifetimes, without ever tiring, or seeking an ending.

I'll keep searching for the lines that make your cheekbones rise, so your smile can always get me high.

I would memorize your table of contents, retain every page like scripture pressed into my conscience.

I am trying to solve the mystery of your identity, unearthing the intricacies of the entity from which you are comprised.

You are the Stonehenge of the human organism, the reason why this Earth keeps orbiting.

God made gemstones the color of your eyes, yet even jewels pale in the presence of your shine.

Your brilliance is impossible to deny.

Compared to you, even Archimedes seems unwise.

Where can I mine the substance you carry inside?

If I found the source, I would be the wealthiest man alive.

Take me to the fountains of your passions, and I will learn to dance to your anthem.

When you speak, you ignite in intellectual fine print, your kindred spirit always shining.

If I planted a tree every time I think of you, we could save the environment.

I have an eidetic memory of every feature you are made of – if there are constellations on land, then you are Ursa Major.

Fragile, yet strong.
Soft-spoken, yet unshaken.
Delicate, and well balanced.
Your heart is honest.

I have a list of everything I have ever wanted – your name is the only one on it.

You are not just a woman – you are a Goddess.

A Land of Ukuleles

I want to take you away, where time moves like ocean tides and love plays a melody on strings of the wind.

We will escape to Coconut Grove, purchase Treasure Trove, and make this estate our home – a sanctuary of sun-kissed mornings and moonlit devotion.

Occasionally, we will drive up to Discovery Cove, to swim with dolphins, to borrow their laughter, and let saltwater cleanse away everything that does not feel like us.

We will unravel life's true calling, scribbling dreams onto seashells, tossing them into waves, watching them return to shore with answers only love could write.

We can beat each other up with kisses, our lips like warriors, our passion an unstoppable lunar dance.

Every day, we fall in love again, guided not by the world's compass, but by the pull of our own gravity.

We will be the ones who prove true love exists, who build castles out of whispers, who fill our pockets with wishes and set them free like fireflies against an indigo sky.

I want to take you away – to love you in every way.

To drink from the fountain of you, taste the waters of your essence, to learn the map of your soul with every sip, every touch, every knowing glance.

I want to imagine forever in a land of ukuleles, to search your eyes like an explorer tracing the stars, wondering how – and why – they shine with a depth that never ends.

We will dance beneath the sky, where raindrops compose our rhythm, where our heartbeats echo into the night, reflecting moonlight, immersed in paradise.

We will stop at every red light, let our lips feel each other up, as they speak in languages that satiate hunger more than any feast, that fill us fuller than any plate ever could, and feed the soul beyond what the body craves.

I want to take you away, to an imaginary land of ukuleles, to paint out the face of our future with the colors of devotion.

I want to snack on your kisses, wake up and realize I was never dreaming – because in this place, every moment has meaning, every breath gets lighter, every love song is ours.

I want to take you away, to a land of ukuleles, where the only crazy we ever find is how wildly, madly, endlessly we love each other.

Happily, forever, in this land of ukuleles.

Celestial Emerald

You are a celestial emerald, a gem so rare the universe folds around you, yet I rediscover you every day as if I have never seen color before.

My heart melts to your touch, liquid light pooling, spilling, cascading toward the gravity of your soul.

I want to fight for your love like a warrior wading through galaxies, battered and bruised, yet glowing from the inside, because surrendering to you is the only battle worth laying down arms in truce.

I want to make your heart melt with love, distill the magma into a potion, and take doses of you until reality shifts, bends, and dissolves, until the walls between us are no longer real, until we, too, become a starry expanse of this luminous green beacon.

I want to decode love's greatest mysteries, offer a college course on the alchemy of us, where the syllabus is written in the fire of our mergence.

I want to be your man, your best, to pass every test, not with answers, but with devotion.

At night when we rest, or beneath the noon sun, and during moments in between, I want to lay by your side, let our energy interlace like vine-covered ruins reclaiming what was always sacred.

With every kiss, we will mist the air with the aroma of our passion, your head on my shoulder, a weight that grounds me but makes me feel weightless all at once.

I would not trade you for all the gold in the world – because gold is finite, and we are ever-expanding, stretching into the fabric of the cosmos, saturated in eternity.

Let's grow into emeralds together, buried deep, rooted in devotion, each facet reflecting the immeasurable love that blooms between us.

We will climb from beneath the roots, burst through earth, and break the surface, glimmering in the rawness of becoming.

You are a treasure, a potent pleasure, a gemstone of the ether.

I want to make your heart melt for me, each drop spelling our names in the language of constellations, each sigh ascending beyond the moon, until our love becomes a nebula, birthing new worlds from our glow.

A love alchemized, transcendent, that drips like eternity itself – a cosmic jade, gleaming with the light of creation.

Eclipsing Illusion

So many weave falsehoods into connection,
mirroring desires they do not embody, shaping
themselves to fit our longing, yet their boundaries
dissolve like mist.

They people-please, soft-spoken echoes of what we
wish to hear, afraid that truth might unmask their
fragility.

They have rehearsed this performance for so long,
self-deception is now a polished craft, a
masquerade of hollow love, a veneer with no
foundation.

But the cosmos does not sustain illusions.

They crash hard when they taste the venom, when
the serpent's fangs pierce through pretense, when
the scorpion strikes unyielding, radiant with truth.

Authenticity is not weakness.

This is the unshakable core of the stars, the
foundation upon which galaxies align, the force
that bends space without ever breaking itself.

You can be gentle and still hold strength.
You can glow softly and still ignite worlds.
Real love never fears being seen.

This union stands unhidden, unafraid – like the
moon refusing to dim, oceans pulling the tides
home, infinite cosmos, forever expanding, forever
true.

Nebula II: Sacred Unions

Love is a force and an alignment, an unfolding, a sacred merging of souls that have always known each other.

In this section, we move beyond the cosmic call of attraction into the ecstatic depths of union.

These poems are woven from the threads of destiny and devotion, where love ceases to be an idea and becomes an experience, a reverence, a surrender to something greater than the self.

Here, passion is both intoxicating and grounding, a force that burns yet soothes, awakens yet softens.

This is the realm of soulmates, of twin flames meeting across lifetimes, of hands that feel like home and eyes that mirror eternity.

These verses embody the celestial alchemy of two energies intertwining, the gravity of hearts pulled into perfect orbit, the electricity of touch that transcends time.

Love is not just found here.
This magnetism is felt, consumed, and forever imprinted in the stars.

Enter, and let love take hold.

Moonlit Vows & Eternal Roots

Not even the most advanced algorithms could
articulate the intricacies of what you mean to me.

No system could synthesize the depth in your gaze,
nor could artificial intelligence render the Soul in
your eyes.

There are frequencies in your presence that would
short-circuit supercomputers.

The sonorous tones of your whispers vibrate in my
fluid like the echo of hymns against cathedral
walls, like ocean waves serenading the shore
under a midnight sky.

The cosmic rays of your intelligence sustain my
cells.

Compelling. Electrifying. Wondrous.

You are a language the universe speaks fluently.

My heart beats like a cheetah sprinting, chasing a
lifetime of devotion to you.

Only a river could flow for as long as your smile is
carved into my being.

I envy the sand that catches your footprints,
the air that weaves through your hair,
the light that kisses your skin.

There are colors in your whispers, spectrums
unseen, spun into the ether of your exhale.

I swim in your waves, letting your essence pull me deeper, yet somehow, even as I surrender, I never drown – I only expand.

An eight-dimensional love.

Untethered by time, where the past, present, and future fold into one eternal moment.

Where devotion does not decay, but transcends form, transcends lifetimes, transcends everything we thought we knew.

My roots entwine with yours, buried deep into the fabric of existence, binding our love to the earth, to the stars, to the unseen dimensions where souls were sculpted before birth.

Moonlit vows, whispered into infinity.

Roots deeper than galaxies, a love expanding beyond lifetimes, beyond the limits of language, at the edge of the eternal expanse.

Starborn Petals & Lunar Tides

Your monumental form complements the grandeur of your essence, a celestial being, draped in the light of nebula-born silk.

You descend from an ancient Gladiatrix, part empress, part myth, with stardust woven through your veins and the cosmos tracing your lineage.

The fervor of your radiance strums the harp strings of Earth, vibrations rippling through tectonic plates, sending tremors through the galactic metronome.

Ferns sway in devotion, bending to the pulse of your breath, as your presence stirs the emotions of the highest cosmic source.

You are the whisper of lunar tides, pulling oceans to kneel at your feet, gravity surrendering to the elegance of your gravitational heart.

Your lips are starborn petals, soft as the dawn-kissed edges of roses that bloom in the gardens of supernova, fragrant with the nectar of eternity.

Your eyes hold the deepest eclipses, where light bends in admiration, where galaxies reflect their secrets in the abyss of your irises.

Your touch is the collision of celestial bodies, a slow-motion stellar explosion, leaving constellations tangled in the creases of my fingertips.

When you move, you are the rhythm of comets in transit, the melody of planetary alignment, the poetry of space unfolding in time.

And I am the tide to your moon, rising and retreating in perfect cadence, forever pulled by the gravity of your existence.

The Constellations Between Us

Your moans are my mantras, a sacred hymn that echoes in my sinew, they ripple through my bones, reverberating into the fabric of the cosmos.

I chant an emulation of your vibration, a whispered devotion, an incantation to the Goddess you embody.

I nurture you with Cancerian tides, cradling your spirit in the soft sway of my moonlit waters, while my Scorpio rises in the celestial temple between your thighs.

My Gemini moon swoons in orbit of the universe of your body, drawn into your gravity, lost in the eclipse of your embrace.

The lines on my astrocartography chart all run directly to you, trailing like magnetic ley lines leading me home.

I bask in the glow of your Venusian smile, soft as twilight's first kiss, brighter than the halo of a morning star.

Your eyes – an entrance to a galactic empress, portals carved from nebula and fire, where time bends, where destinies collide.

I see other worlds when I meet your gaze,
I see our past lives,
our next lifetimes.

The entirety of existence is woven in the
constellations between us.

Celestial Vows & Galactic Devotion

The transmission velocity of my declaration of love for you trembles between the abyss of vastness and veil of mystery.

There is interdependence bridging the sacred core of my allegiance and expansion of our convergence, a cosmic equation where your love determines the orbit of my soul.

Distance will never matter, for you are the master of my devotion, the one who bends time, who anchors me in galaxies unknown, whose gravity holds me still even as the universe expands.

The strongest love potion drips from your lips, nectar that no alchemist could ever recreate, no temptation exists that could pull me away from your kiss.

I will drink your gaze with my soul, let your essence fill my spirit, a flood of light and reverence that courses through me like the Milky Way in motion.

The universe bends to my whispered desire, and still, you are the only one I call into my fire.

I will kneel a thousand times, speak my vows with the force of stampeding elephants, strength of colliding planets, and grandeur of supernovas birthing entire galaxies.

Only you.

I will forever be in awe of the way I see God
through you, the way your light illuminates
what even the stars fail to reveal.

I will ravish you in all the ways you crave, devour
you just as you desire.

With my love, I promise all your insecurities will
expire, dissolving like mist before the morning sun.

The shape of your face, the way your cheekbones
were sculpted with precision, the pride of your
great-great grandmothers etched into your smile –
you carry your lineage with grace, you embody the
strength of generations.

I will protect you like a white lion leading his pack,
Alpha male loyalty, an unwavering force that will
never yield.

You are my North Star, my celestial queen, the
force that keeps my orbit aligned.

And no matter how many lifetimes, no matter how
many dimensions we must travel through –
I will always choose you.

Spagyrical Love

I extracted your essence into a spagyric, dosed on you until we merged spirits.

Then I poured this elixir into African watering holes, and the land came alive in your cadence.

Elephants and rhinos swayed their hips to your rhythm.

Giraffes danced in slow, elegant spirals.

Monkeys mimicked your moans, a primal chorus echoing through the trees.

Lions pressed deeper into their mates, the way I feel you pulse in my bones.

I distilled your pheromones into a hydrosol, dousing barren deserts with your scent.

Overnight, moss unfurled, flowers erupted in bloom, and the land bore offerings of wild berries, sweet with the memory of you.

Ferns curled their fronds in anticipation, swaying to the whisper of your touch.

Now your B12 enriches my cells, remediating the topsoil as well – nutrient and nectar, healer and haven.

Your Fibonacci spirals weave with mycelium, strengthening the roots of ancient trees where white owls sing their nocturnes.

Crepuscular rays stream through the canopy, reflecting the cosmic phenomenon of your form.

Komorebi is most radiant when her light emanates your adornment.

Your microbes are alchemists, spinning tales of playful dragons, flirtatious faeries, and witches who brew psychoactive potions that taste of other worlds.

I am mesmerized by you – every strand, every filament.

I filled an oxygen tank with your breath, sealed myself in a hyperbaric chamber, pressurized with all that you are.

Your air infiltrated my lungs, rewriting my being at the cellular level.

When I emerged, I was no longer the same man.

The bacterial flora on my palms curl around your hands and hold fast.

They know, as I do, how seamless our chemistry is.

Your skin, a temptation, meets my lips, meets my teeth, meets the hunger in my jaw.

I trace the delicate ridge of your labium superius oris, absorbing your essence, grafting your cells onto mine.

Even Horace, poet of love, would be wordless
before this.

You are composed of indestructible fibers, rare as
lenticular clouds, ephemeral as circumhorizontal
arcs – yet permanent in the way you leave your
mark.

You spin me in your web, and I am easy prey.

Willingly, I cross the anchor point, traverse the
radius, and descend into the capture spiral,
marveling at the intricacy of your design.

Clarity in Your Kiss

Clarity is the sensation I feel in my nerves each time my lips meet yours.

When we are apart, I ache for the way your presence stills my heart, the quiet gravity of your love pulling me in, past your strong guard.

Falling asleep with you in my arms, knowing that in this moment, I hold everything I have ever desired.

Purity is the essence of our union.

Merging microbes.
Colliding cells.
Entangled energies.

This sacred oneness with you – a love that expands beyond skin, beyond breath, beyond time.

Our monogamous mouths all over each other's body parts, trace devotion across flesh, whispering vows in a language older than words, we will not stop, not even in death.

Glowing brighter.

Growing deeper.

Rising higher.

Ascending further in love.

Golden Girl

Flowers need a chance too – this is why Earth
stretches vast, so every petal may unfurl, and each
bloom meets the sun.

No blossoms are quite like you.

When you smile, colors are born, hues more mystic
than the fullest moon.

I long to be spun into your cocoon, to transcend, to
see – will we emerge as one butterfly, or two?

I ache for oneness with you.

Each morning, as my hands cradle your face,
my lips will script love onto your skin.

Even the Vatican could not hold your riches.

My golden girl.

Ancient light spills from your shoulders, a glow
traced from the dawn of time.

There are waterfalls in your eyes, rivers of
something holy.

Your heart – so vast, so radiant – must have descended direct from the sun.

The brilliance of your being, the gravity of your glow, lifts me to my highest.

There is no hiding – the way I adore you is written in every breath.

Your Face Is a Treasure

Your face is a treasure, a relic of wonder time cannot erode.

Your smile – the jewels of ancient shipwrecks, gleaming beneath currents where only the brave dare to dive.

Your light is immeasurable – even the galaxies lack enough stars to match the rhythm of your frequency.

Your lips could end deforestation, if only the world saw in you what I do – a force so pure, so life-giving, that even barren lands would bloom at your touch.

Our ally is the truth.

I see her woven deep within your roots, a quiet power, steadfast and unshaken.

The day I met you, honesty and I formed a truce.

Sacred Imprints (For Arlo)

I follow the imprints your feet leave in the sand,
trailing your journey across golden dunes.

I lose sight of you as you crest another hill, but
your laughter lingers – shrees of innocence rushing
toward the vast ocean.

I know exactly where you are.

The chord that connects us is woven thick, a braid
of sweetgrass, unbreakable, fragrant with devotion.

There is something to say about how mesmerized I
am watching you grow.

Each day, I learn more – your strengths, your
kindred spirit, the quiet ways you bloom into
something even greater.

Seeing you, I understand why Mary called her son
divine.

She witnessed the perfection of creation, the
miracle of a child's unfolding.

Is not all newborn life an extension of divinity?

I raise you in a way that protects your purity,
that keeps you from being led astray.

I will always guide you in a good way, contribute
to your ascension however I may.

I honor the sacredness of your psyche.
Life with you is always Irie.

Everlasting Ode

The way your smile imitates an opened rose,
a perfect illustration of your radiant soul.

I could write new verses for as long as my fingers
are tethered to my hands – with you as the muse of
my prose.

The curse and the blessing of professing adoration
to the mysteries of the unknown.

The way your touch hums with the resonance of an
Om, activating the flow of every creative current
within me.

I consoled with the moon – even she stands in awe
of your glow.

I swear under oath, I will love your wrinkles when
you are old, and gaze at you as I do now, while our
great-grandchildren grow.

The warmth of your smile articulates meaning
in a language my spirit has always known fluently.

Perhaps in this lifetime your body is new to me,
but I have held you through countless
reincarnations, effusively.

The way your laugh softens my heart,
how you feel so earthly in my arms.

Jacoby

To Love You Out Loud

When I say I want to be with you, I do not envision our love to exist in secrecy.

I want the galactic confederations and guardians of galaxies to see.

Our union is to be witnessed, written in the stars, carved into time, a love so vivid, the universe turns to listen.

Cosmic forces will hold their breath as I fall to one knee, offering you my all, asking you to embrace forever with me.

Solar flares will scatter the sky in a storm of light, the way your eyes shatter darkness, how your gaze paints my days in golden hues.

As cameras immortalize your glow, the universe beholds your reflection.

On a distant planet, astronomers will have discovered a brilliant new star – not yet realizing this is your soul glowing across the cosmos.

May the first sound I hear as I wake be your laughter, a melody that stirs my soul.

Wrapped in the certainty of you, I surrender to sleep, knowing morning will bathe me in the glow of your presence.

If love could take form, the world would stand in awe of the garden I have grown for you.

Your love grounds me, replacing every shadow with something unshakable.

You gather every stray piece of me and weave them into something complete.

Where uncertainty once lingered, your love builds foundations that never falter.

Your aura is clean, spirit untamed, a fire the astral sea has never named.

You are the brilliance that wisdom bows to, a light that even celestial guides pursue.

Too many mornings, I wake and ache, wishing you were real, not just a dream to chase.

If World Peace Were a Puzzle

I do not play much guitar, but when I think of you, melodies escape my heart like a song the universe has always known.

I am not the best at art, but I could paint your face in my mind – every line, every freckle, and would not miss a trace.

I don't drink, but if your affection were bottled, I would let you intoxicate me with every ounce you've got.

I have not always been the greatest lover, but I know – with you, there will never be another.

Sometimes, I wish we were otters, so when we sleep, we could always hold hands and never drift apart.

If we were albatrosses, I'd soar from the Australian Coast to the Northwest Pacific, searching every seashore to find my mate for life.

I could not be more specific.

If we were wolves, we'd be the alpha pair of the pack, forever loyal, and I'd dismantle every hunter's trap, so you would always be safe by my side when you walk.

I don't know a single piano key, but those eyes of yours – they had me playing all of Mozart's symphonies.

I may be a grown man, but the first time I saw you smile, I felt like a child again, completely smitten.

If only humans could be more like gibbons – when I fall for you, you are the only one I will ever be kissing.

If world peace were a puzzle, and only one piece was missing, I think your presence would fit perfectly – because how could anyone start a war when you bring out so much beauty from inside?

If every person alive could be inspired by the way you appear, we'd witness a million new Shakespeare's, and Romeo and Juliet would happen again every year.

And even if I play the fool, I'll be happy to.

I may not be Copernicus, but my theory is that the sun is centered around you.

Spellbound By You

The color of my shame wears every shade of your eyes – deep as redwood bark, vast as sky before rain.

There is nothing more gigantic than your heart.

Your love is the embodiment of oceans, your essence, the fifth season – something beyond time, transcending weather, surpassing understanding.

The purity of serenity.

Your lips – the end of deforestation.

You are the oxygen this Earth desperately needs, a breath that resurrects, a rhythm that awakens.

With you, I have never been more genuine.

All the colors.

I see you, and I see the colors, where before there was only gray.

Your eyes forced me to confront my demise, to see my undoing and rebuild from within.

I have never held anything dearer than the sacred temple of your thighs.

You look into my soul, when your gaze embraces my whole.

Oh, how I adore every little moan.

I love you with each atom of my being.

You are the antidote to every poison I have swallowed.

I hold your hand and remember the gaze of my father.

You are my forever.
There could never be another.
Your face is my other half.

When I hold you, all I can do is laugh – at the confusion, the hatred, the wars, the genocide.

Because when I am with you, none of this matters.

Mindfulness is your student.
Purity is your professor.

Maybe you are Merlin's muse. My idol. My hero.
My love. My greatest teacher.

My Only Drug

I want to peak inside your mind, trace the curves of your thoughts, inhale the visions you dream.

Can I have a little of whatever you are on?

Your energy feels like euphoria – the kind that lingers, a type that heals.

Can I get a dip of the passion that drips from your lips?

Let me taste your truths like the richest elixir – one sip and I'm lost in the high.

I'd like a dose of that body up close, where every embrace is a rush to the veins, a pulse that sings through my skin.

You are magic in a dying world.
An untainted remedy.
A potion that turns gray into gold.

I am not asking for your number, I seek eternity.

Will you just be my girl?

I want my chest to be your pillow, and I hope you drool while you sleep – because the more of you I have on me, the better off I'll be.

The scent of your breath is my favorite intoxication.

The weight of your limbs is the gravity that keeps me whole.

I do not need a hit of anything else – you are the only drug I ever crave, my only addiction.

Your Auric Sphere

I was a faint flame, contained by my surroundings, my potential to magnify obscured by a void still unknown.

You were the oxygen I needed to ignite, to brighten.

There is a force you carry that overpowers doubt, a strength you exude that breaks through stone.

You elevate my sense of worth, inspire me to feel vibrant.

Now, I am the Phoenix Rising.

Compatibility was defined the first time the vermillion border of my mouth pressed against your labium superius oris.

Even Horace, the poet of love, could not express in
verse the alchemy I felt – like an alchemist
extracting ormus from intentions that are pure.

This universe orbits around your auric sphere.

When our lips meet, gray whales breach, and I
breathe in each of your exhalations – the experience
of oneness.

A merging of city culture with a man of nature.

We ascend to the sacred spaces of imagination.
Intellectual penetration.
What I feel for you goes beyond adoration.

My thumb traces the patterns of your phalangeals,
and clasped against mine, your fingers feel like a
part of my hand.

Whoever said attraction never lasts knows nothing
of what we have.

Your touch hydrates my skin like raindrops on
drought-stricken soil.

I soak you in, pores like sponges pulling you as
close to my core as I can.

Every fabric of my being wants to be your man.

Your energy saturates each atom like moss
spreading across the trunk of ancient redwoods.

You have always been all that I need.
The antidote to my disharmony.

You enrich my dreams.
Your sweetness nurtures the roots of my purity.

There will never be a more pristine smile.

Your teeth are like diamonds, reflections of
sunbeams.

I was caught off guard by my own reflection gazing
back at me as I affixed my stare to the depths of
your iris.

Our union is righteous.

Not even the deadliest virus could replicate the
power of my devotion to you.

You are the most desired Goddess.

If I could run across the world for you, I would win
every race.

I would sacrifice my freedom to wake up to the gentleness of your face.

There is nothing more delicate than your embrace.

No culinary flavor could ever satiate me more than the way your kisses taste.

Your beauty makes a leopard's rosette coat seem ordinary.

No other woman could ever compete with how much you mean to me.

I rise to your soul effortlessly, the way piano keys hammer each string.

My inner child keeps asking if I can bring you to school for show and tell.

There are no acoustic melodies yet to be played in sync with the way my heart beats for you.

No pastel ever made could emulate the colors you expel when you break the shell.

No lens manufactured could capture the resolution of your light.

You are the ambassador of my vibe.
Nothing gets me more high.
The way you look at me amplifies my shine.
Your beauty is more potent than the sun is bright.

The depth of your essence brings Merlin's magic back to life.

I know for certain – you are the woman whose admiration I will give my all to earn.

Behind the curtains of your external image, I see your inner worth.

I hear the voice of your tenderness speaking in a language I will always know.

You make any house a home.

Your foundation is the substance of what I stand for.

I hold you close to my center and never want to let go.

You are the source of my creative flow.

A tsunami could not extinguish the fire you ignite in my soul.

Disarmament

I am drawn to you as fragrance is born of flowers, as petals unfold to kiss the wind, as sweetness drifts unseen, yet leaves a presence everywhere.

I love you like ants carrying the impossible, small but mighty, lifting burdens with purpose, building homes, nourishing life.

Like rain feeding rivers, I gravitate toward you, a current I cannot resist, swimming in your waves, surrendering to your tide.

My adoration for you – the sun illuminating infinite sky, a boundless glow, a warmth that never dims.

Like the way a son looks into his father's eyes, searching for wisdom, finding love in reflection.

I will curl up in a cocoon with you, wrapped in our becoming, and emerge as one.

Your love disarms all guns, turns steel weapons to dust, melts war into whispers.

The high I get from you outdoes all drugs – no substance could ever compare to the elevation of your embrace.

Your hugs unplug the violence in this world, short-circuit the chaos, tame the winds.

The way your touch softens my heart is how dawn tenderizes the edges of night – a quiet, unstoppable peace.

The Soul Before Form

"Everyone is a moon, and has a dark side, which he never shows anyone." – Mark Twain

I was alive preceding the heartbeat, prior to sound, in the dawn of form.

This life force activated me, pulsing through my embryonic stillness, an energy unmatched, garnering celestial consciousness.

I was already here, before I listened with ears, when my breath was still a whisper in the void.

I sensed the aroma of redwood soil ahead of when I had a nose.

I touched nature all over her body before I had fingers, earlier than nerves – beyond the veil of when separation existed.

I saw the perfection of forests and oceans, admired colors now extinct.

I have always been immersed in the never-ending beauty of this Earth.

I loved you in the echoes of chainsaws, when trees still stood high.

When Grandfather Moon lit the sky so bright, we could see mountains for miles.

Glaciers stretched as wide as your smile.

You enchanted my soul, back when grass was not buried beneath pavement, when mines still held precious metals locked in time, when no hands had yet defiled the land.

I admired how untamed and wild your spirit's flame was flying.

I was watching – ancient to haze or pollution, before heavenly orbs became ghosts of what they once were.

Back when stars were simply reflections of your love.

Nothing got me higher.

Foregoing bombs, factory farms, and guns, there was a world bathed in the warmth of a sweet and friendly sun, shining out on everyone.

Your love.
The disarmament of war.
The patterns of your phalangeals.
The way your grace fills me with purity.

I watch you fly, wings like eagles, scattering seeds into a world freed from greed.

"The gem cannot be polished without friction, nor man perfected without trials." – Confucius

And yet, you shine unpolished, uncarved, untouched – a gem that needed no chiseling to be divine.

To Build a Trust with No Lock, Only a Key

We somersault around each other's hearts,
spinning like constellations in a cosmic waltz,
our devotion exalting the heavens
with a love that neither time nor tide can sever.

Our merriment dissolves the weight of the world,
marching to the beat of our own parade, our spirits
so radiant no rain could ever dim our shine.

Our alliance is unshaken – a truce unbreakable, a
love unshakable.

We put the ghosts of past lovers on a noose and let
them hang, vowing ours never turn out the same.

We hold each other close, and yet, we let each other
go – knowing that no matter where we roam, we
always return home.

Across oceans, over miles, we speak through cells,
our essence traveling beyond sight, our bond
unshaken by distance, our love immune to time.

I do not fret about what you do while you are
away, because our foundation is firm.

If we respect where we stand, we can be the
world's most beautiful woman and man.

I understand your concerns.
I will fill you with every bit of love you deserve.

Let's build trust with no lock.
Knowing we are each other's key.

We can work around the clock and use our
adoration to drown out fatigue.

When I hold your hand, our feelings are freed.

We manifest our brightest dreams.

When you breathe, I want to sleep in your rhythms.

When you whisper, I want to feel you, not just
listen.

Your essence is absorbed into my heart, like
sunbeams into the earth, your love – an energy, an
orbit, a pull.

Our devotion is stronger than the Great Wall of
China, a fortress against all deception, a sacred
empire standing taller than the lost pyramids yet to
be found.

They do not crumble.
They do not fade.
Like our love, eternal in every age.

The good stuff that cannot be found, the truth that
will never unwind.

Because there is no lock – and we are the keys.

Even if we sail across seas, you and I will remain loyal to our bond.

We will resist deception.
We will build a pact that never ends.
We will be the world's lesson.

Baby, you and me – we are the blessing.

The Tree We Grew from Stardust

I breathe the rhythms of your heart, inhale your pulse like the first light of dawn, and exhale, knowing distance is an illusion woven by time, which has no hold on us.

Our foundation is intertwined with mycelial roots.

As they burrow deeper into Earth, our love blooms, tangling, twisting, reaching, weaving us into patterns of the fabric of existence.

We climb the tree of life we have created, branch by branch, hand in hand, wrapped around each other like ivy drunk on divinity.

We never let go, grasping the infinite garden of us.

I want to listen as your thoughts begin to whisper, winds carrying your serenity like sacred hymns written in nature's breath.

Every moment stretches forever.

The pact we build transcends the known, etching into the ether.

Through vistas of infinite possibilities, we are explorers, lovers dissolving into love.

Like rivers carving valleys, we continue our course.

I want to decode the constellations in your gaze, to map the galaxies behind your eyes – because I swear, nothing has ever been more cosmic than this.

That look – the one that never ends or fades, unravels me, makes a thief of my soul, tempts me to steal you away so we can build forever out of rainy days.

I fantasize of you and me, laying lazy, falling into madness, making ourselves crazier over each other, because there is no other way.

We are roots, translocating nutrients to our tree, voltage radiating from the storm, biophotons beaming from sunlight.

Daughter of Starlight

I remember when your presence made me feel like no matter where we stood, I was always home.

I think about those moments when we synchronized our breath so effortlessly, each inhale carrying your spirit into my bones, warming me with the kind of purity that no treasure could match.

Each exhalation released another ounce of reservations I had always kept bottled inside.

Memories linger of a thousand smiles, shared beneath rising suns, under clear blue skies, through thunderstorms that roared like ancient hymns, and under moonlight that hummed us to sleep.

Your eyes are celestite, carrying the wisdom of a sky that has existed since before time had a name.

They reflect a beauty that can only be seen in the deepest embers of the Atlantic, where secrets of the cosmos are whispered into the lull of the moon's calling waves.

Oceans flow through you, your aura painting the air in colors that never existed before.

From the very first moment, I looked deep into your soul and understood my purpose.

I accepted my role – the father of a being
woven from light itself.

I knew then where my heart belongs.

My love for you is the definition of sincerity.

The harmony of your laughter is the nectar lining
the petals as flowers bloom just to honor you.

Your voice is a song ancient redwoods sway to,
a melody that carries through branches touching
the heavens.

When you were born,
my brother Darin finally found his peace.

I know with all his great, big heart,
he wished he could rewrite time, take back his
choice, just to meet you in person.

Your name spells heaven backward, and if heaven
is real, then your innocence is the gatekeeper,
filtering out all doubts, opening the gates to
warmth and radiance.

All my life, I tried to find the perfect description of
beauty.

Only after your birth did I finally decipher the true
meaning.

Nebula III: The Fracturing Light

Love is radiant, yet even the brightest stars collapse.

This section is a descent into the spaces where love unravels, where devotion is tested, where illusions dissolve like constellations swallowed by the void.

Here, we face the raw truths of betrayal, heartbreak, and the aching silence left behind when something sacred is severed.

These poems are written in the echoes of what once felt eternal, in the hollow chambers of promises unkept.

They speak to the moments when trust is fractured, when love slips through trembling hands, when the weight of absence feels heavier than presence ever did.

Even in sorrow, there is wisdom, and in heartbreak, there is revelation.

For love, even when lost, does not truly die, but transforms, teaches, and carves new space within.

This is where pain does not seek vengeance but understanding, where wounds are not curses but catalysts, where the breaking is also the becoming.

Step into the twilight of love's undoing, and let the fractures illuminate what remains.

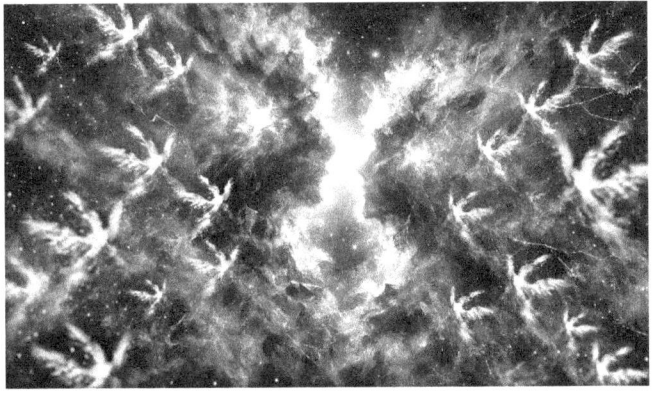

Scorpion's Oath: A Vow Written in Stars

Loyalty is when the scorpion stings you, and your only response is to sharpen her aculeus, so that even in your absence, she may still defend herself.

As venom seeps into your veins, you resist the instinct to recoil – instead, you gently cradle her telson, ensuring she will store this misrepresented panacea, this fatal cure, for all future men who dare to earn the honor of winning her Antares, the brightest star in the constellation Scorpio, and essence of her heart.

While gasping for your final breath, you stare into the center of her carapace, searching for a reflection of the love she once poured into you with all twelve of her eyes.

You recall the sacred dance, the moment your bodies converged, as you entrusted her with the sanctity of your seed, delivered into her spermatophore, so she could draw from your offering, so she could create lineage from devotion.

Even as your pulse weakens, you offer her the last of your hemocyanin through her spiracles, so she may circulate what remains of your love.

A final gift – so that in her book lungs, your spirit will forever live.

The venom deepens its reach, and yet, as you salivate profusely, you recognize this sensation – the same hunger you have always felt when waking beside the most desirable woman you have ever known, trailing kisses down her face, her neck, her body.

Your breath shallows, yet she immerses herself in your exhalations, savoring the last of your pheromones, finally grasping how much she never wanted to live without them.

Numbness creeps in – a sensation long familiar, mirroring the starvation of love that led you here.

But then – the chlorotoxin in her venom begins to work, dissolving the cancer of life without her.

The bradykinin-potentiating peptides regulate your blood pressure, just as her embrace once steadied your nerves.

The hyaluronidase proteins whisper to your cells, reminding them of how completely you accepted her – every facet, every flaw, from her rage to her resilience, her walls to her ability to conquer all.

And as your life wanes, for one final moment, you see her wounded inner child – the one she has hidden behind plated armor.

You gather her in your arms one last time, cradle
her like a vow, and whisper –

*"I would do anything to erase the traumas
that made you shield yourself from the love
you have always desired."*

The Judas Kiss of Blooming Trust

You spoke my name like roots whispering to rain, swore your body knew before your mind did – that my lineage would rise from your sacred womb, like sweetgrass bending to the breath of God.

And I – like a mycorrhizal promise beneath ancient oaks – spread my essence to your soil, pulled water from the depths, translocated my love into the marrow of your being.

But what is love to the Judas tree? Blooming magenta with false hope, promising fruit where none will ripen.

What is devotion to the cuckoo? Laying love in another's nest, letting foreign wings hatch a story that was meant for us.

Your beauty demands perpetual vigilance – I gasped at your magnitude, at times staring into Aetheris too long, as if the weight of your presence was something only gods should carry.

I stood in awe, watching divinity take shape in your form, not knowing celestial presence can walk away.

Now you are the Ephialtes to my Thermopylae, guiding the enemy through the pass, letting daggers find my back where only my trust should have rested.

I was Brutus' embrace before the blade.

I was the thirty pieces of silver before the noose was tied.

Soon, other pheromones will replace mine.

The familiarity of my touch, the taste of my kisses.

And in these moments, my scent will rise in your memory like an unshaken ghost, murmuring of the strength once wrapped around you – undeniable.

You will recall how my lips etched eternity into your skin, how their fire left embers no time will cool.

The rhythm of my presence, the gravity of my sway, the intelligence of my mannerisms, will haunt you in ways no other ever could.

Revenge is the language of the broken, but silence is the dialect of the divine.

So, I will be the forest without a path of return.

I will be the temple whose doors are closed.

I will be the purple hyacinth, whispering only of regret in the garden you can no longer enter.

When you wake in the arms of another, when your breath catches in your chest, and you reach for poetry that is no longer written for you.

When the absence of my warmth feels like winter settling into your bones.

May you know the weight of what was lost.

May the wind carry my name in the spaces between your ribs.

May my silence echo louder than any sonnet I ever wrote for you.

Alchemy of Angels and Demons

Beelzebub was once an angel, until his environment poisoned him and his essence collapsed into shadow.

Angels and demons are not opposites – they are the same entity, simply fed differently.

When an angel is poisoned, they do not vanish – they mutate.

Their vibratory rate is reduced, the impurities they ingest solidify within them, nourishing their spirit with darkness.

But change the environment, purify the blood, cleanse the morbid matter from the terrain of their being, and the angel resurrects.

The organism remembers holiness.

On a cellular level, this is pleomorphism – the transformation of life.

Place a healthy organism into an acid medium, and the cell morphs into an aggressive pathogen.

When returned to an alkaline state, function is regained, restoring balance, returning to light.

The same law applies to the human organism.

When one depends on synthetic drugs, pills, and processed food, they mutate, their sanctity obscured.

When they cleanse and purify, they shine again.

We are not required to see everyone only in their light.

To call people out when they are out of alignment is an act of love, to remind them – with truth, not indulgence – to return to their center.

The weaponization of decency instructs us to bite our tongues, to withhold truth so as not to offend.

But silence is complicity.

This false kindness allows the descent to continue, enabling the downward spiral to inevitable demise.

Yes, love can conquer demons – but how often do we see people harm in the name of love, confused by their own distortions?

To love in a way that empowers is to be direct, to be unafraid to trigger, to risk discomfort to ignite transformation.

May we work collectively to elevate the frequency, by choosing authenticity over appeasement.

Rather than inflating egos with words they long to hear, may we challenge those we love to confront their own incongruencies – so they may rise, purify, and return to the divinity that was always theirs.

Sonorous Shadows

Sound moves – carrying echoes of fate, whispers of what was, vibrations of what could be.

Gasps claw for breath, witnessing freedom stripped away with the strike of a gavel.

The noises of innocence vanish as mistakes unravel into evidence, thread by thread, unraveling the fabric of redemption.

Wishes for another chance – lost in translation, drowned in the silence between what was meant and what was heard.

Prayers ricochet off steel bars, off concrete walls, pleas for mercy that never reach their destination.

Longitudinal waves of laughter entwine with the wails of disaster, an orchestra of grief and grace playing on an indifferent current.

Susurrations of inaudible gestures ripple outward – vibrations unseen, too obscure to be heard, yet too powerful to go unnoticed.

Whispers of first hellos collide with echoes of last goodbyes.

Euphonious inflections flicker in the gaze of a lover before the connection declines, before the final note fades.

The residuum of closing 'I love you's' haunts the corridors of memory, a refrain unable to be silenced.

Faint undertones of "I want you back" play on cordless currents, keeping us fixated on the past.

Crumbling castles dismantle as royalty falls, as thrones are abandoned to rewrite destinies.

To abdicate the crown in pursuit of redemption.

To surrender the past for the renewal of will, for the chance to rise again.

Enslavement births revolutions.
Struggles resurrect solutions.

Impossibility is an illusion.
Freedom is translucent.

Discipline of Letting Go

I once loved a woman with all my soul – the freckles on her skin, constellations mapped in flesh, each microbe, every cell, the unspoken rhythm of her being.

I am at peace knowing that I was brave enough to open myself completely, to surrender in devotion to someone through whom I saw God shine impeccably.

I dared to risk the fallout, the repercussions, the residuum of love lost.

To accept what seems illogical, to master the art of letting go – this requires a discipline few are willing to learn.

To walk away when every pulse within me knows she is the one I long to hold – this is an act of rebellion against my own conscience.

I imagine the way a tree feels as the axe hacks into her trunk.

The sound of gunshots to an orphaned fawn.

A harpoon piercing the chest of a gray whale.

The drying of rivers where salmon once spawned.

Still, somehow, I convince my spirit to carry on.

Just as birds continue to sing in fallen forests.

Like Earth, even after being severed, still finds a way to bloom again.

All this strums a familiar melody, reminding me – I am empowered by everything.

Falling Through You

Love was the night I saw my first shooting star, the way you looked at me – my wish was already granted.

Your gaze was enough to make sanity go crazy, to pull the tides from shore, to untether me from logic and let me drift into you.

Love is a labyrinth, a tangled game that strangles the world, leaving us breathless and raw, twisting hearts into knots we spend a lifetime attempting to untie.

Love is your body on mine, time dissolving into breath, just passion – the friction of longing.

Tongues twisting around energy, your breath entering my lungs, my soul exhaling back into you, a cycle, a current, a fusion that makes us one.

Love is your smile – like Christmas morning sunlight reflecting off snow, warmth of family wrapped in closeness, the glow of something too pure to touch, but too beautiful to look away from.

Love is unity.

If only you knew the depths of what you do to me, how your presence has rewritten my existence.

Love is an angel in flight, wings outstretched into the infinite, climbing to a place where no boundaries exist, where time bends to the weight of what we feel.

Love is the first look you gave me.

I swallowed your astral stare whole, devoured the fire in your eyes, like an elixir that could keep me alive forever.

But love – love escaped me.

Your Shadow is the Past

You turned your back and walked away,
your silhouette dissolving into the horizon.

As distance grew, I could feel your pain ripple
through the air, like smoke from a fire still burning
somewhere deep inside you.

I searched for ways to bend time back into our
arms, to stitch the seams of love that once fit like
silk, but somehow, the thread unraveled, the
frequency shifted.

I watched you walk, your stride uncertain, like a
melody played in reverse.

Listening to the sound of your footprints, as
familiar as the rhythms of my own heartbeat, the
wind threading through ancient trees, the echo of
my name in your voice.

I tried to speak, but my utterance was swallowed
by the weight of a heart burdened beyond the reach
of reverberation.

Love stains.

The permanence of a heart that breaks leaves an
eternal mark on our innocence, etching memories
into the fabric of our soul.

We are carried to faraway lands, then abandoned there, stranded in the wilderness of confusion, wandering between the past and an illusion of forever.

The illusion defeats us.
The elusive glimmer shatters.

I held on for as long as I could, cherished our kisses like artifacts from a lost civilization – until the day came when I had to let them turn to dust.

Love makes us strong, but loss is abusive.

We get tempted with new beginnings, opportunities that shimmer like mirages, promising renewal, but never quite tasting the same.

Yet, even in ruin, the soul remains unshattered.

Your shadow is the past.

I watched you fade into the tide of time, while I remained in the sun's embrace, released from the grasp of fading phantoms.

Where Stars Fall, We Rise

When we first kissed, passion blossomed like flower petals unfolding in slow motion, daffodils perfumed by the essence of your pheromones, innocent love germinating in moonlight.

When we made love, you aroused me like MDMA dancing in rain clouds on sunlit afternoons, a high so pure not even the strongest doses could match this level of intoxication.

No force could faze me, no reality could awaken me, from the way your touch rewrote my existence.

I held you close, letting creativity provoke my imagination into dreamscapes of romance, our spirits fastened, woven into the fabric of something timeless.

We watched the stars fall, hands clasped,
and I swear – they were made for each other.

I could lay with you forever.

Even if the Earth shattered, I would gather up the
pieces of our love and stitch them back together.

I would travel the broken forests, swim through
waves of defeat, collecting every fragment that ever
mattered, never letting them escape my reach.

Like the emptiness that swallowed me whole when
you traveled a separate way.

I let you go so we could meet again another day,
on this impossible pursuit for the so-called love we
spend our lives fighting to attain.

Life Without You

I rolled out of bed, trying to avoid the weight of an empty pillow.

The indentation of where you once lay, a ghost of warmth left in the fabric, reminded me that absence has a shape.

I let go of the comforter that still carries the scent of your skin but no longer holds the promise of return.

I watched the sunrise, but beauty now feels like a betrayal, like a lover's kiss that vanishes into mist, a Judas moment where light exposes the hollow space you left behind.

I broke open my morning coconut the same way your departure split my heart in two.

The top scoop, once your favorite, remains untouched – a gift that now feels like a wound.

I picked the best pomegranate kernels from the cup, sliced the ripest pitaya – but the first cut, the one I always saved for you, tasted like something stolen from my own soul.

I chewed around the pit, the same way life eats at my core without you.

I asked the nutrients of our favorite smoothie
to piece me back together, to blend this ache into
something that could nourish instead of
destroying.

I stepped outside, barefoot, charging with the
Earth, feeling soil press against my soles, thinking
of the massages you gave me, how they once
grounded me in love.

In sweatpants, and a t-shirt that was mine but
always looked better on you, I searched for the
comfort I once had – this longing that exists only in
memory, lingering in the creases of time.

There is no replacement for you anywhere.

Jasmine spring and rose heaven only smells right
on your skin.

Our journey cannot be over when we have yet to
bloom again.

I wear the rejection you gifted me, reading over
cards you once inscribed with love, words once
etched in certainty, now abandoned like fallen
leaves.

Why should we move on when we fortify each
other?

This weakness erodes me like a slow tide on stone
every moment you are gone.

I drove to the forest to visit the trees,
hugged the weeping willow, and she asked,

Where is your light?
Where is the one who set you free?
The one who taught you how to love so deeply?

I walked miles through mud and memory, trying
to purge the sadness that seeps into my bones like
rain.

But your face appeared in the sun, your smile
haunting me like the echo of gunshots to an
orphaned fawn.

I live with this ache from dusk until dawn, and the
shadows of longing creep back in all night long.

I stopped for groceries, self-checkout became self-
reflection, how I was always so mindful to get you
the snacks you desired, and juices you required,
now discounting the cost of solitude.

Even with perfect vision, I feel blind without you.

Love was never a game to me, but a sacred
covenant.

My loyalty does not wane, only grows through the
cracks of absence, pushing through concrete,
reaching for any light left glimmering.

I picked up the guitar, strummed the melodies
my spirit still sings for you, remnants of ceremony
songs woven into our story.

I prayed for answers.

I meditated to release the sadness metastasizing through my blood.

I practiced yoga to stretch beyond the confines of grief.

I opened my chakras to welcome a fresh current of healing energy.

I released my insecurities.

I tried to let things be.

I tied my ego to an anchor, dropped my attachments off the cliffs into the sea, watched the waves swallow my resistance.

I lied to myself – insisting we were not aligned, but honesty pulled me back, whispered in my ear how perfectly we fit.

A part of me died the day we met.
That part was loneliness.

You revived me with love.

The longer I wait without you, the more I know – you belong by my side.

I may not be perfect, and I do not always do things right, but my love for you will never fade.

You will always be my sun, my gravity, my guiding light.

Even in absence, you are woven into my being, your essence etched into the fabric of my soul

The warmth that lingers, and glow that never dims.

My love for you remains long after the stars have burned out.

Nebula IV: Alchemy of the Wound

Pain is not the end of love – disheartenment is the crucible where love is refined.

This section is an exploration of transformation, resilience, and the wisdom that blooms from suffering.

Here, wounds do not remain wounds; they become gateways, teachers, sacred offerings to the journey of becoming.

Through heartbreak, we discover our own capacity to heal. Through betrayal, we learn the truth of loyalty.

Through loss, we understand how to hold, release, and trust in the cycle of renewal.

These poems exist where pain meets revelation, where sorrow does not consume but transmutes into strength.

Like stars collapsing into black holes only to reignite as something greater, we, too, are remade.

This is the place where fire does not burn but purifies, where the broken pieces are not discarded but reassembled into something divine.

Enter the forge.

Let the wound make you gold.

Jacoby

Strength of Sovereignty

The potency of a man's strength is not in his ability to conquer, but through the grace of his gift to love.

Power is indicated in his capacity to forgive, willingness to compromise, and steadfastness in holding onto sovereignty in a world that conditions him to seek validation outside of himself.

When pain arises, freedoms are stripped, and the heart is shattered – how do we expand our love instead of closing off?

If our children are taken from our embrace, when hands dare to pull apart what love has bound, what do we hold within that keeps the fire alive, yet burns with grace and gentleness, flowing still, in a state of love?

When we are betrayed – by friend, lover, or blood – what is required of us to truly forgive?

To release the weight of emotions misaligned with harmony.

Can we see the one who wounded us not as an enemy, but as a child – aching to be loved, longing to be heard, desperate for someone to see them, to acknowledge their needs?

Are we strong enough to hold ourselves
accountable for the roles we played?

To thank them, forgive them, and honor the
divinity within all?

When conflict arises, the bravest thing we can do
is to face it directly, to seek resolution, not ruin.

Yet, how do we compromise if we are not receiving
what we seek in return?

When we embody the knowingness that life will
bring us what we need – we move toward love,
not with desperation, but with purity.

Peace is always greater than confrontation.
Calmness dissolves chaos.
Love humbles those who seek hate.

If something does not go our way today, we trust
this will cycle back when we are stronger, wiser,
and more prepared.

To remain sovereign is to reject the voices that say
we are not enough.

To say no to propaganda.
To elude the programming.
To dodge fear, hysteria, and division.

Sovereignty is knowing – we do not need to tear
others down to rise.

We do not look strong when we gossip.

We do not appear righteous when we pretend.

We are not powerful when we betray our own nature.

When we stand as we are, with no need for masks, and no hunger for approval, we exude strength – onward, upward, and inward.

Alchemy of Letting Go

Microbes slowly eat away memories, digesting the remnants of you, until your name dissolves from the archives of my hippocampus.

The parasites that once stirred at your presence, that once clung to the sweetness of illusion, begin to perish.

There were organisms within me that thrived solely on the weight of your betrayal, consuming the energy I once poured into your hands.

I felt them, misplaced – like an elephant in the room, a quiet recognition of how I tolerated deception in the name of love.

But even they will fade, like footprints washed from the shore, like false promises evaporating with the air they were spoken into.

The moment your gaze tried to snatch my soul, I should have known – that love does not require theft, that eyes should not deceive when they claim to see me.

My kidneys excrete what remains of you, purging traces of every moment you welcomed others into our sacred space without my knowing, without my consent.

Slowly, my creativity returns.

The rivers of my mind no longer clogged by the residue of what was never meant for me.

My nerves reignite, pulse steady, lungs open to the air that was always mine to breathe.

There is no anger, only transformation – the kind that turns decay into fertile soil, where something beautiful will bloom.

I return to myself.

Remedy for a Wounded Soul

She is every inch of embodied woman,
woven from threads of divinity and fire.

Her hair – luster spun from celestial light,
combed by the breath of the cosmos.

Her teeth, faceted diamonds, a constellation of
brilliance behind her lips.

When she smiles, the world is silenced,
mesmerized, as if witnessing the iridescence
of the Great Barrier Reef.

Her eyes, twin pools of royal blue tang,
shimmering with the depths of unseen oceans.

When she speaks, the air bends to listen,
captivated, as if the wind herself has found a muse.

She moves with a rhythm both primal and refined
– part seduction, part grace, a symphony sculpted
into form.

Even the trees lean closer, swaying to the melody of
her laughter.

Vastness expands where her presence lingers.

In her embrace, there is no way for a soul to be
empty after.

If there are angels on Earth, she is clearly their
master.

Rose Petals & Purple Sage

I am who I am because of you.

Your imprint – an eternal ember, a legacy carved in the quiet corridors of mystery.

I see your silhouette in the wind, whispering secrets through trembling Aspen leaves.

Glistening mountaintops drink your light, the brightest star ever to rise.

Wrongs unravel into right within your presence, the hue of life woven into your essence.

The spectrum of creation glows in your cheeks, cosmic radiance sculpting your being.

Hercules bows, knees pressed to the dust, humbled by your strength.

The length of your smile outpaces light, bending time with sheer brilliance.

You are the embodiment of devotion, a sovereign soul, a deserving wife.

Glacial melt kisses your skin, flowing rivers of renewal.

Your taste – ambrosia that quenches the unseen, hydrating souls with nectar of the divine.

A single drop carries the blueprint of Eden, sprouting heaven upon Earth.

There is no scale to weigh your worth.

Levity defies gravity in your presence, goodness rising in every breath.

Coral ignites beneath ocean waves, a hymn in the language of light, singing your name in endless chorus.

You are always the answer.

The sprite queendom dances in your tides, their laughter laced in the foam.

An ancient jewel, hidden in the marrow of mountains, waiting for the world to remember.

Redemption resurrects in your grace.

The gatekeeper wears your face.

Your womb – the sanctum of creation, where time folds into infinity.

Your art drips golden honey in the hollows of my heart.

Your spark, an ember that never fades.

Rose petals and purple sage, you are the way.

Echoes of A Father's Love (For Nevaeh)

I know one day she will appreciate my unique ways and be proud of who her father is.

When I show up to her soccer games barefoot, walking across the field, she won't feel embarrassed by my nonconformity – she will acknowledge my quiet defiance, a reverence for the earth beneath my feet.

There will come a time when my long, curly hair is no longer a tangled nuisance in her eyes, but a symbol of wisdom, a thread woven through lineage.

She will no longer call my head a rat's nest, maybe instead, she will admire the way I care for every strand.

Perhaps one day, she may even want to put braids in for me.

I envision the times when I return from long travels, and she runs to meet me – her face beaming with excitement, her arms eager to embrace.

For now, I will accept her solemn, half-hearted greetings.

I trust that the sharp words she throws at me will help her release whatever needs to leave her heart, so that kindness may fill the spaces instead.

When she scolds me for slurring my S's, perhaps this will remind her to accept the way people speak, to find beauty in the rhythm of different tongues.

For as much as she dismisses my knowledge, as much as she recoils at my healthy ways, I know she carries my wisdom with her.

A seed planted – which, one day she will water, soon, she will bloom.

She may not admit, but I know she will remember how I remain in my center, stay calm, keep her safe, healthy, and protected.

She must like my silliness, the way I make her laugh, how I sing to her, and play songs on my guitar – even if she rolls her eyes, even if she protests.

On my last visit, I watched her walk into the store with her mother, and an overwhelming euphoria washed over me.

I smiled in awe, honoring the miracle of life, the beauty of watching her bloom into the radiant young woman she is becoming.

Her long legs, flawless curls, bright, resplendent smile – a reflection of her mother, a reminder of love, a testament to time.

And I am grateful.

Lessons in Ash and Bloom

Constellations strum broken guitar strings, trying to mend the hollow sounds of life without you.

The sound of gunshots to an orphaned fawn.

Harpoons piercing the chest of a mother whale, while her calf watches – silent agony swelling in the tide.

A thousand stampeding elephants flattening what I once understood as love.

I made a pillow of ancient redwood ashes – the remains of a white owl's home, clear-cut to the ground for reasons no man will ever know.

Then, I hugged the last black rhino.

The disease of excess.
The sickness of always wanting more.

Now, I learn from mycelium, weaving life around decaying bones, composting artifacts of Kardashian culture, picking up shattered pieces of what I once thought were morals, but now know are my values.

I carry them with me into the unknown.

What I do know – Great Spirit loves us all the same.

New life always rises from manmade fires, no matter how wide they spread, no matter the acres they consume.

Soon, the moss forms again.

Bees make honey where wars have crippled mankind's dignity.

And one day, a sapling bears the sweetest fruit – her roots laced with genocides, yet she refuses to let circumstance become her reason to stop blossoming.

Lost languages are found again in places we never thought to look.

I thank the trees for teaching me resilience.

I honor the waves for washing away the things we will never understand.

What Cannot Be Lost

In the distance, there is a dissolvement of difference.

From afar, we open our hearts and listen.

The energetic flow of two souls, playing telepathic harps.

I always see your glow in the dark – no matter how heavy the night, or how deep the silence.

You are the reason the rooster still crows each morning, the sweet sunshine that blankets our skin after every storm.

Wolves howl to the void, even as their packs diminish to the weight of human ego.

Separation exists, only so we may find each other again – in solitude, surrender, and sacred reunion.

We trust in Godspeed, honor divine plans, even when we do not understand.

We embrace loss and celebrate what can never be lost.

Frost reminds us of how powerful our warmth is within.

We may be worlds apart, yet our spirits script the same verses, transcribing what we already know – without lips to speak, without ears to hear.

I could walk a thousand miles, sail to uninhabited islands, and still – your energy exists.

Unfinished Strokes

There she is again.

That feeling taunts me, lurking in the brushstrokes
of memory, haunting the canvas of my mind.

Your look is sultry, a slow burn that never fades,
a heat I can feel even when your presence is
nothing more than an afterimage.

I can never get enough.

These thoughts never end.

Even though you have gone, and I have tried to
cleanse my mind of your hues, you remain.

There is not enough sage in the world to burn away
the residuum of your energy that will always stay.

I want you so much that your absence is louder
than the moments I held you.

You are daunting to watch, a beauty so fierce, I feel
you integrating into my vision, without permission.

I painted you once, but the colors ran.
The lines blurred.
No pigment could hold you still.

Even now, your eyes refuse to be captured, your
form dissolves into shadow, your essence spills
past the frame.

Some muses are never meant to be contained.

Jacoby

Peace Treaty

I kissed your teardrops and swallowed your hurt, never missing a moment to transmute pain into sentimental sincerity.

I tasted your discomfort, and my body became your shield, developing antibodies to fight off the plague that was eating your beauty alive.

I devoured your sickness and transformed poison into protection, woven from the fabric of galaxies.

I debunked medical science and revived you back to life, pulling you from the depths of a sorrow that once threatened to consume you.

I took deep breaths for you, pumping oxygen back into your lungs, exhaling life into your spirit.

I sacrificed my temple to restore your divinity.

I opened my heart to unlock yours.

I loved you immensely, offering the only cure your soul ever needed.

Now, you are free to be the bird you always were, spreading your heavenly wings, feathers synchronized with the wind's sacred rhythm.

I helped lift you above the clouds, so you could erase everything that ever tried to pull you down.

I gave you the key to my soul, so you could always dwell in the serenity of my being.

I saved you from darkness simply by shining my light.

My twin flame.
My soulmate.

The final piece to the puzzle of my heart.

My adoration for you is starlight.

Every night, I see you in the moon.

Old Growth Forest of Your Soul

I am desolate, in a crowd of beautiful people,
searching for familiar eyes.

I feel isolated in cities built of misunderstanding,
where voices clash like waves, against the jagged
edges of what we once called truth.

Emptiness fills me, on this planet dense with
conflicting visions of what life should be.

I scavenge the damaged ethnosphere,
searching for the old-growth forests of your soul.

Pieces of enchanting memories echo in the
serenade of your laughter, filling the void where
your presence once was.

I still hold you in fairy tales of undying love, where
passion ignites like a thousand tiny suns, reflecting
in the rhythm of your heart.

I inhale your butterflies, exhale forever, under
meteor showers of never-ending affection.

I watch an abundant night sky, constellations
strumming broken guitar strings, trying to mend
the hollow sounds of life without you.

A galaxy of stars still does not shine like the aura
that surrounds your muse.

With every flower's new bloom, I see your smile.

Your pheromones are nature's perfume.

And in the distance, I feel closer.
Separation molds us into abundance.

On this remote island, with only darkness, I find
hope in the light that our memories hold.

I am sailing into the perfect storm, knowing that
when the confusion settles, you will teleport back
into my arms.

We will evolve into organic farms, our immortal
sorrows feeding happiness to the children of
tomorrow.

The bond we share will last forever,
nourishing the soils.

Peace will grow at the roots of our unity.

In another universe, Gaia tells love stories of you
and me.

Eternal Return

I cannot summon words vast enough to capture the pull of your presence, the scent of your spirit, or the way your essence bends reality.

But I can send you my love in currents unseen, vibrations rippling through the cosmos, until we meet inside the ethers where no boundary exists.

We journey through midnight caverns, beyond planets unnamed, past the borders of what was once real – scaling each other's hearts like the tallest mountains of an undiscovered world, only to fall, together, into an ocean deeper than the abyss itself, where light still finds a way to reach.

How come your love never fades?

No force, no moment, no distance – there is no parallel, nothing else in existence, that can hold up against the weight of you.

I gave you my oath, I committed to forever, and no silence, no storm, not even you could pull me away from the gravity of what we are.

Why do your eyes turn miles into moments, worries into whispers, storms into stillness?

I would drown in your love just to wake up in another lifetime so I could search the planet to find you again – to prove that out of billions, you are my only one.

The earth will tremble when my knee touches down, when the weight of never letting go crashes into the ground.

After the losses, distances, nights spent searching the stars for signs that we were still written in them – I look up and see you.

The rest of me.

Not as a dream, or as a memory, but as the constant the universe always knew I'd return to.

Soul Never Dies *(For My Brother Darin)*

I hear your isolated tears falling gently to the dirt.

You are part of the soil now, you climbed your way back into Earth's womb.

Some say you arrived too soon, but I know, you were seeking a way to heal wounds too deep for this world to mend.

You left with no fear, crafted the only lasting cure.

Now, you are pure.

No more court mandates or medications, no more prescriptions forced down your throat.

You chose your last sedation, a final sigh into eternal unification.

The train tracks carried you to liberation.

I know your mind was held hostage by psychotropic pills, your will silenced by chemicals that were never meant to heal.

You were part of a medical experiment you never agreed to join.

Yet you endured, for nine long years, held steady in prescription storms, fought through the torture, the pain – and even in leaving, you empowered me more than you will ever know.

Maybe you didn't mean to go as soon as you did.

Maybe, in another timeline, you would have stayed.

But we accept your decision as is.

The courage to face that train – was your only escape from the fate of a psychiatrist's negligence.

Now, you are everywhere.

That shooting star.
That electric pulse in the sky.

In the movement of the wind, the hush of the ocean, the rustling leaves – I see your silhouette in all things.

Maybe you are walking on the moon, or the butterfly emerging from her cocoon.

Maybe you are the mysterious flower waiting for the sun to rise, so he can bloom.

I feel your rhythm in the blues.

I wonder if you visited the redwoods first, or made your way to the forests of Peru.

And though the grief runs deep, I know – freedom was always waiting for you.

Please don't cry anymore.
Let the skies do the weeping.
No more pain.
No more shackles on your brain.

No more trying to fit into a system that was never
built for you.

Now, you can dance, and the skies will rain.
Now, you can fly with unbroken wings.

You are everything now.
That bolt of lightning.
The drops of rain.
The luster on a lion's mane.

I feel your energy all around.
The sun is now your soul.
The roots are your bones.
Earth has become your throne.
The universe is your home.

I see you walking in the distance.
Hear you talking.
Feel your presence.

You discovered the miracle drug.
Learned how to rise above.

Your spirit helps me understand the meaning of
love.

You are everyone now.
I see pieces of you in each who passes by.

A part of you glimmers in Nevaeh's light,
your strength shines through Arlo's might.

Your smile never dies.

In your eyes – there was always that look of oh,
how I wonder why.

I still hear you laughing.
Could never forget your voice.
Feel you tremble.
I know you had no choice.

An angel started a new life.

But you still walk by my side, teaching me not to be
blind, guiding me past the propaganda, leading me
into the light.

Maybe you were a Messiah in disguise, the magical
child within who only wanted to be recognized.

The Messenger

She swooped in, landed on my shoulder – a shadow of knowing, a whisper from another lifetime.

There was a heart on her feathers, a message woven into the ink of her wings.

The colors she wore changed me forever.

December sun, overcast with gloom.

I looked into her soul, recognized her before words could form.

She had seen too much.

The weight of atrocities etched into the weathered lines of her face.

She carried the ghosts of a world bleeding beneath greed.

She had nowhere to go.
Loggers took her home.
She was not alone.

I, too, had been torn from my own.

She told me of the last rivers drying, of water poisoned for livestock, oil, and gas, of forests reduced to memory, of mountains blasted from the skyline.

She spoke of the skies – no longer blue, painted thick with chemical trails.

Trying not to cry, I confessed – we humans created this mess.

Gaia gave us dominion, and we failed.

We cut down the forests to raise flesh for profit, never knowing we could thrive on grains, seeds, fruits, and roots.

We suffocated rivers with chemicals to heat our homes, while the sun waited, untouched, ready to warm us all along.

We stripped the Earth of hemp that could have healed, bled the mountains dry for resources we never truly needed.

She listened.
She rested.
She stayed, until departure felt best.

Now, the stars shined for her,
casting light across her obsidian vest.

I watched her fly back to the moon, wings spread like depleted uranium, deformed Iraqi children, Afghan and Palestinian men and women screaming for peace.

Snowflakes fell at my feet.
Toes buried in cold redwood soil.

Temperatures cannot hide true warmth.

Clouds wept frozen tears, nourishing the roots of a
world still waiting to bloom.

A feather fell from the sky.

I am not the rightful owner,
but I will carry this gift for now.

Her residue stains deep like molasses.

That blackbird sang,
and her voice was magic.

Nebula V: Wisdom of the Stars

Love, when fully lived, does not leave us as found.

Our experience transforms, expands, and reveals what was once unseen.

A force that breaks, light that mends, and rhythm that carries us forward, even when we do not yet understand where we are going.

This section is an arrival. A place of reflection, integration, and transcendence. Here, love is not only something we feel but is also something we become. The language of the stars, wisdom whispered through time, and universal knowing that pulses through galaxies and hearts alike.

These poems speak of love not as possession, but as presence. Not as longing, but as awakening.

They remind us that love does not fade; but evolves. Love is written in the orbit of planets, breath between lovers, and in the silence of knowing.

Love is not just an emotion, but is also a way of seeing, a way of being, a way of moving through this world and beyond.

Here, under the vastness of the cosmos, we do not chase love. We embody the emanation.

Step into the expanse. The wisdom of the stars awaits.

Reverence & Renewal

I am grateful to harbor the art of expression, to transmute thought into words, to channel light through voice and verse.

With this gift, there is no limit to the change I can generate.

Too many confuse power with control, abundance with greed.

They manipulate generosity, and weaponize compassion, waging wars that dim the radiance of beauty on the planet we call home.

No resource is renewable when the life force surrounding is extinguished.

Each tree is an oracle, a sacred vessel offering unique blessings to a universal whole.

Every inch of land, all oil reserves, and each body of water, gives more in health and harmony than when stripped, sold, and bled for profit.

I am grateful for diversity – in biology, culture, language, race, in every nuance that composes this mystic and enchanting Earth.

Those who poison the space we inhabit are not worthy of leadership, of notoriety, of prestige.

By honoring their confusion as acceptable, we anchor ourselves in the same sickness that fuels degradation and destruction.

I am grateful for the strength of will, for peace of mind, for the ability to make choices that solidify my place in the ocean of growth.

A tide that rises to awaken a sleeping species, one being brainwashed into believing there is nature in extinction.

We are failing on the highest level.

Biocide, ecocide, genocide – all expanding at the hands of man.

Chemicals evaporate into Wall Street surges, dissipate through the atmosphere, and infect every corner of the world, bringing darkness, disease, decay.

I am grateful for food that grows from clean soil, for nourishment that does not require suffering.

To know my diet inflicts no wounds is to know that my spirit is free.

By releasing my attachment to consuming suffering, I elevate my own well-being while breaking the cycle of harm.

I am privileged to live in awareness, to be conscious, to be present, to see beyond deception and recognize the vastness of culture, language, knowledge, and love.

I can always learn more as a student of endless possibilities.

There is no room for confusion in a mind seeking beauty.

This illusion of ideologies that fail stagnates movement, until I expand beyond the limitations that try to confine me within a universal mind that fears evolution.

I am in harmony, rewriting the scriptures of the meaning of being human.

Through spirit, I acquire all that I will ever need.

I feel freedom with each rhythm my heart beats.

I am thankful for my lungs, for breath untainted, for my blood flowing freely, pumping truth through my veins and endothelium.

The Greatest Wonder

I had a dream where I was given the gift to travel this world and witness every wonder in a single journey – to chase the divine, seek the extraordinary, to uncover the greatest marvel known to humankind.

I stood before the ancient pyramids of Egypt, and they towered above me, far grander than I had ever imagined.

The smooth limestone had long been stripped away, yet 4,600 years could not erase their magnificence.

Even in ruin, some beauty never fades.

I followed the zig-zagging spine of the Great Wall of China, snaking through the mountains, stretching beyond the horizon.

I learned that over a million hands had bled for this construction, thousands of souls lost in the creation.

All difficult tasks, I see, come at a cost.

I beheld the Taj Mahal, a palace of poetry sculpted in marble, a masterpiece appraised at a hundred million – and yet, not the greatest wonder.

Still not the thrill I sought.

I longed for more radiance,
for something beyond the stones of kings.

So, I ventured to the Serengeti, where life moves in great waves, over a million creatures colliding, hooves thundering, earth trembling – the greatest animal show on Earth.

But even this – did not complete my satiety.

I found my way to the Galápagos, where evolution paints each creature anew, shaping beings found nowhere else on Earth.

I stood upon Espanola, the jewel of the islands.

I wandered Santa Cruz, where giant tortoises roam, watched sea lions tumble through Fernandina's waves.

Yet even this – the raw miracle of life itself – did not match the greatest wonder I sought.

The Grand Canyon was not as extravagant.

I ascended Machu Picchu, stood where the clouds kiss stone, but this presence did not match the potency of standing before you.

I thought, perhaps, I had to leave this world.

So, I voyaged to the edge of the Earth, Antarctica's icy spires rose against the sky.

Where penguins scurried across frozen kingdoms,
and stillness hummed with ancient whispers.

I still could not find one thing to affix my gaze,
the way your eyes hold mine.

I stood before Iguazu Falls, where Devil's Throat
roared with the might of the heavens.

The deafening crash could drown a man's soul, but
all I wanted was something quieter, like how your
cheeks illuminate with the ancient glow of the
morning star.

I sailed through the Amazon, where rivers weave
through tangled forests, where every breath tastes
of life – and yet, I realized I had already been to the
only place where I want to be.

I wandered through Bali's emerald terraces, so lush, impossibly green, yet nothing was as photogenic as the way you first looked at me.

The Great Barrier Reef, teeming with 1,500 species of fish, dancing with whales, dolphins, and sea turtles – still, not the greatest wonder.

I reached Bora Bora, a paradise cradled by an extinct volcano, a turquoise sanctuary so spectacular I almost believed the place was not real.

And yet – nothing is more natural than the way you first looked at me.

The way I surrendered to your essence, not through force, not through effort – but with ease.

Then I awoke,
still in a dream,
sleeping beside you.

I realized that even 4,600 years could not erase the way I feel about you.

Yes, there will be struggles.
Of course, we will go through storms.

But the price we pay for love is never measured in time.

Even a hundred million could not buy your smile, your charm, the way your mannerisms make life feel abundant.

I was reminded – life, in the fullest form, is simply you and I.

There is no island as rich as your lips.
No stars are as bright as your eyes.

No extravagance, no treasure,
could ever out-measure your kiss.

After all this – the pyramids and glaciers, jungles and reefs, mountains and golden temples, I discovered the greatest wonder.

The greatest wonder is how God crafted a woman so delicate, so exquisite, so marvelous.

And somehow – He placed her in front of me.

Jacoby

Luminous Guardian: The Bodhisattva's Light

Your ethereality is an antidote to the misuse of weapons, a reminder that goodness outweighs greed, that deeds rooted in love will always rise above actions fueled by emptiness.

The way you take pride in your convictions, how you share your potent charisma for all the world to witness – shapes the future and heals generations so that war and poverty never find a place in their DNA.

A true teacher.

A professor of wisdom and wit, one who leads armies of potential, guiding them to embody gentle strength, deep compassion, and the kind of love that accepts without condition.

Your guidance is what we long for in those who raise the next light bearers.

Among all leaders in this galaxy, you stand at the Brahmin level, a true Bodhisattva, a channeler of mystic messages, conduit for angelic activations.

Your value oscillates between immeasurable and incomprehensible.

You, standing fully in your power, is among the greatest gifts humanity has ever received.

So, let us bow to your greatness.
May you always know your worth.

May you always emanate
the luminous lamp of beauty
wherever you go.

May your humor and generosity
continue to fill hearts,
lighting the way for others
to awaken.

Ethereal Embrace

I see your iridescence unfold in your expressions,
rainbow exudations dancing with your essence,
light bending to the contours of your soul.

Your irises – cerulean blue, colors I never knew
existed until I saw the cosmos reflected in your
gaze.

Your flower petals bloom in the brightest hues,
pigments only the heavens could have painted.

Your phosphorescence is the very embodiment of
presence, your opalescence a living scripture
etched in the language of light.

I watch your incandescence spill from every
element of you, illuminating the path that leads to
your ascension.

Your pheromones – a marriage of rose heaven and
Jasmine Spring, an ambrosial offering blended to
absolute perfection.

I honor the ancient light woven into your
deliverance, the celestial code etched into your
existence.

You transmute my challenges into teachings,
expanding my capacity to hold and become love.

You sculpt ecstasy from the delicate weaves
of my identity, stitching your presence into the
seams of my existence.

I feel you in my cells.

Your kisses mean the trees to me, roots entwining, branches reaching, leaves whispering your name in the wind.

You are the force that turns darkness into poetry, that sculpts the stars from mere reflections of longing.

You are the reason the universe knows how to shine.

Yemaya

You are the bride of the star's luminescence, keeper of tides, weaver of currents, and breath of the ocean's eternal hymn.

With a crescent's pull, you call the waves into motion, whispering secrets to the moon, casting silver trails upon your sacred waters.

Your presence carries me in flight, buoyant upon your embrace, a rhythm only the soul understands.

Your essence – Most High, a divine song woven into the waves, a hymn of sustenance, of birth, and boundless renewal.

Whales sing your praises, their voices like prayers that roll beneath the surface, echoing through time, telling stories older than land.

Dolphins speak in tongues not meant for human ears – ancient languages, syllables spun from other galaxies, transmitting the wisdom of stars through rippling light.

Your blues – deep as the womb of creation, as vast as the gaze of my beloved's eyes.

You are the keeper of all things fluid – the spirit of surrender, the force of forever.

Yemaya, let me be your wave, let me rise and fall with your unbroken grace, let me dissolve into the infinity of your tides.

Hieroglyph

To replicate your light would be impossible.

Edison tried ten thousand times – a halo spun in threads of white – and failed to ignite.

Your glow ascends to untold height.

Scientists scour the elements, relentlessly pursuing this gold that only emanates as your aura.

Your brilliance brings Luminaires delight.

Engineers marvel at technology, yet if they attune to the frequencies of your heart, this world will birth inventions that shine beyond the veil of sight.

Your existence is ancient art.
A story written before time could start.
A masterpiece sketched in the Cosmos' heart.

I have seen you etched in hieroglyphs, painted on cave walls in lifetimes before this.

They inscribed you as a guiding star in endless night, the beacon that wise men followed with celestial might.

Those sages, those mystics, they paved this path for you – knowing you were chosen to guide lost sails to shore.

I swear, the night sky was rearranged the day you were born.

A new constellation formed – a wisdom bathed in sacred insight, etched into time, whispering your name.

A luminous vow that shall never wane.

True North

She resembles an orb – a celestial body that never
wanes, a glow neither time nor distance can dim.

Her presence is an etching upon my soul, an
imprint more permanent than stone.

She is a shield against cruelty's sharp sword,
her warmth dissolving the frost of old wounds,
thawing the places where my heart turned cold.

My true north.

The light that beckons me home, a compass spun in
golden threads.

The glimmer of her smile coaxes forth my inner
child, where innocence and wonder are free to
roam.

Her laugh – beguiling.

Her energy – tantalizing.

An inexorable pull tugs at my core, realigning me
when I drift too far.

In her presence, I return to center, as if the universe
itself designed her as my axis.

She is the greatest gift one could ever receive, the
gleaming force that could bring any man to his
knees.

A muse so divine, that artists would forsake their fortunes just to glimpse her radiance.

I could be shackled, bound, cast away – yet the sight of her face would still set me free.

Even honeybees grow envious of the potency of her nectar, for there is nothing in this world more fragrant, or sweet.

Curse & the Blessing

You are the universe – both a blessing and curse, a force fierce and tender, woven from stardust and verse.

Your evolution is not loss, but the unfolding of your worth.

A chrysalis unraveling, a destiny written before birth.

With time, you will come to see – you have always been an invaluable facet of the divine, the unshaken brilliance that no shadow can confine.

The genius who ignites the poet's wandering mind, the muse whose presence turns mere words into rhyme.

Qi In Concert

Your body is a divine instrument, weaving melodies of elements.

Strum the strings of your soul, let your heartbeat keep the tempo.

Urge your voice to sing, a hymn of truth, a chant of being.

Tap the drum, let the rhythm of your pulse echo in canyons of memories that can never be undone.

Elongate those hums, let them vibrate through your bones, a resonance felt in ancient tones.

Shake the maracas of your Qi, let your energy dance like wind through sacred trees.

Express love not just in word, but in a symphony of your being.

Golden Nectar of the Soul

"The shield of a courageous warrior is recognized by the dents."

Let honey live in your heart, this sweetness sticking to the way the world perceives you, and permeating through your art.

Allow yourself to be pollinated by so much kindness that all you know are smiles and laughter, that every step you take blooms with the fragrance of compassion.

Let empathy root in your essence, deep as the trees, wide as the sky.

Receive the earthly and celestial blessings that serenade your soul – branches swaying in whispered hymns, ocean breezes carrying prayers to your skin.

And may your spirit become the quiet force that keeps others breathing, that reminds them of a love still lingering.

Jacoby

PachaPapa

PachaPapa, have you been hiding?

We summon you – return to us.

Mama cries for your presence, for your hands to mend what has been broken.

She needs your strength to dismantle dams, to free her rivers once more, so her waters cleanse what has long been lifeless.

She calls for your might to guard endangered trees, to stand as a wall between destruction and the origins of sacred geometry.

Stagnation in our streams has become a breeding ground for corruption.

Subversion of nature has unleashed chaos, hatred, and malevolence.

Will you stand for us?
Will you speak for her?
Intercede.

Help us disarm missiles, silence bombs, resurrect peace that was always meant to be.

Show us the way to abandon drills, to dismantle this command-and-conquer mentality.

We need your wisdom to decompose the poisons –
the chemicals, the pesticides – so our food may
pulse with life, so insects and microbes may thrive
again.

All wars end at home, within the family unit,
from hands that prepare meals, and arms that
embrace a child.

From gardens bursting with nourishment, voices
that speak with tenderness, fathers who honor,
mothers who remember their worth.

Broken vows birth shallow morale.

PachaPapa, we summon you – teach our men how
to cherish, how to nurture, how to provide.

Let us remind our women why we are worthy of
their honor and respect.

Erase antiquated paradigms, for these never-
ending feuds are illusions.

Harmony is not a dream – this is a serene scene
within reach.

Earth Father, unify us.

Build a bridge between the stars.

Raise an impenetrable shield to guard the values
and virtues that protect and conserve.

Cast away all that does not serve goodness.

Invoke clarity, return us to purity.

Let mycelium devour the landfills, returning
wasted riches back into your core.

Guide us to detach from darkness.
Let struggles dissolve like mist.
May our minds be cleansed of fear.

Lead us closer to Source.
Open the portal to higher order.

Let the Earth Guardians and Gatekeepers reclaim
what was lost.

Guide us back – to music, to song, to art.

Collapse corporate curriculums, so schools may
teach nature's laws.

Let all poisons be cast away.
Let us remember presence and play.

For violence has an antidote – that reverberates
laughter.

We know this as love.

PachaPapa, hear us – let humankind once more
embody the light of Christ Consciousness.

Jacoby

Reexamining Value

We have been conditioned to measure worth by what can be owned, treasures that tarnish, and things that rarely last.

But what if the greatest wealth is not something we can touch?

What if you – your presence, your spirit – are of the highest value?

What about love? Connection? Meaningful relationships?

Consider the miracle of conception – when two souls collide to co-create life, when a child gazes into our eyes, mirroring our mannerisms, learning the rhythm of our movements, offering unconditional admiration before the world teaches otherwise.

Remember the first kiss with a lover, the moment you finally feel held – after years of navigating wounds left by abandonment, fractured families, betrayal, and struggle.

How that feeling lands in every cell – a revelation, a reckoning – knowing you have found someone to share your beliefs, passions, and secrets with.

Falling asleep entangled in them, waking to their breath against your skin, their warmth dissolving old fears.

Drool on your face, microbes mingling – a strange
and sacred nourishment.

Then, drifting back into dreams, rediscovering
childlike innocence.

Loyalty growing like roots in your heart, devotion
stretching beyond words.

The initial spark expanding – fueling the violet
flame that enshrines us in divine protection.

What is more valuable than authentic connection?

To exist in a love so sacred, so unwavering, that
jealousy cannot enter, because we honor the divine
orchestration that brought us together.

To have real friends – the kind who will travel
hours to help, who listen without judgment, who
show up in the ways we require our parents to.

And in turn, to become the present, undistracted
parents we once longed for.

What about fresh air?
Pure water?
Lakes and rivers to swim in?

Sunlight pouring into our eyes,
blanketing our skin in warmth.

The exhale of the emerald giants,
standing for centuries,
watching the world shift
while never questioning their worth.

This is an invitation –
a call to reexamine what we hold sacred,
to shift our gaze toward the treasures
that no currency can buy.

Phoenix Rising

She ascends beyond elements, into the Divine,
beyond limits of imagination, unbound by
boundaries of time.

Her Spirit melds with the Soul of Christ, an
embodiment of nature untouched, unfractured by
man's estrangement from wholeness.

Pure being – a feeling indescribable, a power
resurrected from within, once silenced by the
weight of forgetting.

But now, she remembers.

She speaks with elevated confidence, her voice is a
force – potent, unshaken, clear.

The awakening of something ancient, something
primal, something true.

No longer will her beliefs be confined.
She has stepped into the dissolution of disparity.

Clarity has torn apart the illusions woven into her
culture's fabric.

Through her regenerated lens, a new earth
emerges.

She is a seer of colors that once lay extinct.

Birdsongs flutter through her thoughts, soft
melodies reshaping her mind.

She hears the melting of struggles, the dissipation of hatred, the surrender of conquest and control.

Her wings bloom, lifting her through the cosmos, a mutiny of senses, a rebellion of light.

She is vivacity bursting through the most fertile soil, rooted in the truce that sustains equality.

A reconciliation of goodness and light.
The cessation of combat.
The collapse of division.

She is the harmony that silences war, the balance that fends off tyranny.

She is the Phoenix Rising.

From the ashes of malice, her radiance rekindles the beauty of life.

Kundalini Fire

There is substance only light knows, glowing through your radiance.

Your shine heals all ailments.
The divine strike of your eye stuns even hatred.
You demand love every way you walk.
A cultural awakening roots in your power.
Strength needed to empower nations.
Lost knowledge waiting to resurface.

The only key to unlock the peace we all seek rests within your being.

A celestial leader.
One of Gaia's finest teachers.
Pachamama is in awe of you.

Her trust is embodied in your touch.

She draws life from your kundalini fire.
You raise the global frequency higher.

You inspire brightness in a way even the devil admires.

I Am a Tree

I am a tree.
I simply absorb.

My ancient wisdom whispers through rings of time, teaching generation after generation without ever speaking a word.

I take on storms, drink the rain, and stand unshaken through seasons of fury and grace.

I am home to bats, owls, ravens, hawks, eagles, vultures, and macaws – winged prophets that rest in my arms.

Black jaguars sleep with me, silent guardians in the night.

Gorillas, apes, chimpanzees, sloths, and orangutans swing from my branches – limbs intertwined with theirs, partners in time.

Insects depend on me.

I am their sanctuary, their universe of movement.

My imagination is free.

I partner with levity to defy gravity, lifting rivers through my veins, guiding water upward toward the sky, where my leaves breathe life into the world below.

Fungi weave their magic beneath my roots,
delivering nutrients from my core to the entire
plant kingdom.

I charge in the moonlight; I grow in the sun.

I withstand the coldest winters, always smiling,
knowing that spring will come again.

Wildfires burn my bark, but never my core.

My soul is light.
My trunk is love.

I dance with the wind, swaying to songs older than
ancestral blood lines.

I am beautiful.
Pachamama is my queen.

Gaia's Unfinished Symphony

She radiates a frequency that even peace longs to touch.

Her soul harmonizes with compassion that only love truly understands.

The foundation of her being is built from the substance that the tallest trees inhale, the breath that makes forests sing.

Her heartbeat is light, pulsing in rhythm with rivers, tides, and wind whispering through canopies.

Life persists – as microorganisms and mycelium, as smiles and soil, as sunlight and water woven into the fabric of an ancient, breathing Earth.

Yet, the pigments of a colorful planet fade into the shadows of war, a darkness that, if left unchecked, threatens to swallow dawn.

An army of unconscious allies competes to witness the world's demise, their indifference ingrained into the hollow chambers of a universal mind losing to greed.

Wars dismantle every rising sun.

Gravestones of slaughtered culture wash upon every shoreline, etched with echoes of voices that no longer speak.

Guns turn strength blind.
Bombs over Gaza and Mosul.

Rivers run out of room to cry.

These dams are blocking freedoms, forcing tides into silence, while oil pipelines steal the ocean's breath.

But mindfulness matters, even in a world that pretends there are borders, where divisions are drawn in blood, even where truth drowns beneath the weight of forgotten waves.

Because Gaia still beats beneath us, and her frequency cannot be silenced.

Unchained From Illusion

Today, my soul feels free.

No longer confined by cultural delusions, stereotypes, or political confusion.

My mind climbs like levity, defying gravity, as rivers run up spines of redwoods, pulling wisdom from the rings of time.

I feel my spirit slipping the noose of modern technology, eluding expectations that buried my childhood in a labyrinth of dead ends and shattered dreams.

Today, I found satisfaction in raindrops piercing hilltops, in the warmth of clouds blocking my vision, but never the sun.

I laughed myself to tears remembering the barricades I once thought would keep me trapped.

I cried myself to awareness, leaving behind the doubts that sabotaged my purpose.

Today, I danced with shadows one last time, letting them slip into the graveyards where my failures lay to rest.

I stopped planting seeds and became the soil instead, rich with wisdom, fertile with confidence, establishing roots where warped thoughts once stood their ground.

I watched thick layers of ignorance drown, and felt no guilt for refusing to dive into the circus of lies that manipulate a blind society to watch their potential wither through foreign lenses plastered to their eyes.

I painted my own democracy with an untainted imagination, the sacred gift of creation.

Today, I stabbed temptation with the sharp blade of my inner strength, burying my misunderstandings in untapped mines that will never be exploited.

I welcomed nature as my God, kissed heaven all around me, found divinity in flowers and trees, and showered naked in waterfalls of dreams that once dried up from lack of opportunity.

Today, my feet sank into unity, mycelium threads massaging my soles, syncing my pulse to the rhythm of the wind.

Now, when I breathe, I inhale love.

Hope fills my lungs, trusting others will wake up, and rise above the pollutants pulling them down.

Today, I stopped competing for a place in a world built on fragile egos, and instead, I mastered the art of becoming myself.

I whispered to my ambitions, promised them that
these synthetic walls would one day collapse,
that freedom would find us, aligning with passion
like the sky kissing the horizon.

I noticed the animals in cages watching us through
iron bars, wondering why we choose to stay locked
inside social constructs no different than theirs.

Today, I found a leader trapped beneath layers of
fear.

He had been suffocating in held-back tears, buried
under the plaque of years spent consuming the
poisons manufactured by greed.

I flushed my system of the lies of civilization,
cleansed my conscience of the mistake I made as a
kid – trusting history books, believing the doctors,
praying to the monster hiding under my bed that
they call the American Dream.

Today, I donated my failures to my past, mapped
out my future with fresh, untamed visions.

I made a pact, to always do first, what the lost souls
put off until last.

Today, I grew my angel wings of the raven,
discovered the black jaguar that had been waiting
inside me all along.

They carried me home to the forest, to the source,
to the truth, to the essence of my being.

An Anthem for Soul's Revolution

There is a soul resting inside this beautiful instrument embodying my being.

Her essence captivates light.

His presence beams through my pores.

Skin glowing like fireflies, emanating life force, uniting the masculine warmth and feminine strength into something whole and untouchable.

The love flowing through this body, spirit, and mind is a psychoactive drug, altering fiction into reality.

Fairy tales transmute into forest trails, leading me to enchanting places, where I create lasting relationships with magic faces carrying auras from worlds beyond the illusions I was raised to believe.

I refuse to sleep through the extinction of races and cultures.

I chase the dream of diversity, where freedom is not a commodity, where separation does not sever our chance at world peace.

Wars sabotage the livelihood of Earth.
Court systems batter our paths to grace.

The real battle is within.

We must conquer our own temple, find glory
without gold, power without chains, freedom
through meditation and meteor showers of self-
satisfaction.

I have wings that help me soar above the storms
drowning ambition, and claws that pierce the
chains anchoring so many into shallow graves.

I will not be buried or silenced.

My bark has been burned and scarred,
but beneath the char, my soul remains unharmed.

The stab wounds from women's spirits waiting to
be found could not break apart this white wolf's
heart.

Pain befriended me – a never-ending mending
of being misunderstood by lost objects pretending
to be affectionate, but too afraid to be authentic.

My soul and I, climbing through trenches, refusing
to be buried beneath the ashes of weakness,
honoring the connection between my roots and
branches, protecting the core that keeps them from
breaking – the same way love prevents the world
from ending.

Awareness is an eternal blessing.
There is no hiding from the truth.

Currency is an illness.
The cure is talent and sharing passion.

Mainstream kills, tightens the noose around the neck of innocence.

There is no way to trust a truce with ignorance.

When education is manufactured from arrogance, all we learn is doom.

My soul aches for what schools cannot teach, for what no reverend has the wits to preach.

I want to know what preserves my ability to love, so I will never be tempted by propaganda, hatred, cultural conditioning, envy, guns, or drugs.

I want to break open every orifice of tenderness, launch an Apocalypse of Awakening to kill the anger, racism, confusion, and revive the music of lost generations – the songs silenced by soldiers programmed to lose.

Command and conquer has drilled so many holes that we are now burying our survival inside an emptiness that is the only thing left once the profits vanish.

How do we fill the voids of neglect, abuse, betrayal, and abandonment – without laughter, happiness, true love, real friends, and unbroken families?

My soul exists to prove that competition is a tragedy, we all have the capacity to free ourselves from material fantasies, and that love is the only entity that will rescue this galaxy.

Anatomy of Our Roots Entwined

We are not leaves caught in passing winds, or fleeting petals that tremble at the breath of time.

We are roots – deep, deliberate, unshaken – spinning tendrils through eternity's soil.

I see you as my root cap, guardian of my tenderness, shielding the fragile beginning of all we are, softening the earth before me, so I may press forward unbroken, so I may grow unafraid.

You represent my apical meristem, genesis of my becoming, where love divides, expands, multiplies, pushing ever deeper into the sacred unknown.

Each kiss, a cell splitting into infinity, each vow, a silent promise whispered into the dark.

You are my zone of elongation, great stretch of my devotion, where we do not remain still, but extend, lengthening toward the core of one another, anchoring love beyond surface touch – beyond momentary passion, into forever's pull.

You evolve into my zone of maturation, lover of many forms, where I do not merely love you, I learn you – every curve of your being unfurling into purpose, every breath sculpting into something sacred.

As my root epidermis, you shield me against drought, absorbing what the world cannot give me,

pulling in waters unseen, feeding the places in me
that once lay barren.

You are sustenance, you are survival.

You, my cortex, my keeper of memory, where love
is not just lived but stored, where the echoes of
every whispered name pulse through the marrow
of us, where your touch lingers even when your
hands are gone.

I honor you as my vascular cylinder, conduit of life,
Xylem of loyalty, Phloem of devotion, carrying all
that is pure between us, circulating the essence of
our sacred bond.

You flow through me, I flow through you – no
ending, no edge, no escape.

And when storms rise, when winds howl, when the
world would try to unearth us, you are my lateral
roots, expanding, gripping, holding, so that no
force, no famine, no flood could undo what we
have become.

We are not love that withers.
We are not momentary.
We are not transient.

We are the taproot – deep, unwavering, sovereign.

A single force, bound in divine architecture,
reaching not just for each other, but for perpetuity.

Wisdom of the Earth & Sky

The love I have for these forests is the same love that Sky Woman carried as she descended to Turtle Island, cradling seeds that would birth the fruits of our existence, our sustenance, our becoming.

This is the life force of co-creation, the pulse that germinated the conception of my children, the sacred rhythm of all that breathes, all that knows the song of life.

Like a lioness milking her cubs, teaching them the jungle's whispers, this love nourishes, this love protects, this love instructs.

A wisdom that moves like mycelium, weaving unseen beneath the earth, delivering primordial knowledge, transmitting sustenance, uniting the queendoms of plants and trees.

This adoration roots me in dignity, holding my values high, preserving the sanctity of my purity.

I inhale, and the air that fills me is the breath of the cosmos, the sacred exchange between self and sky, the pulse of the universe pumping life into my core.

I see love in the way the wind carries seeds, how rivers quench the earth, fire purifies, and roots bind the land together.

I cherish this essence, not only in my devotion to nature, but in the way I walk with compassion, and offer generosity to all I meet.

To love you is to love the Earth itself, for the same force that draws me to you is the one that moves the tides, shapes the mountains, and paints galaxies across the night sky.

The spirit of these trees expands the soul within me, teaching me that love is not only what we feel, but what we become when we surrender to the wisdom of the stars and soil, the sky and sea.

Epilogue: Where Love Becomes the Universe

Love is not confined to words, nor bound by the fleeting moments we try to capture in ink.

We write of the great force that moves galaxies into dance, that bends time into poetry, that breathes fire into passion and music into silence.

Love is the cosmic thread woven through every constellation, the invisible melody playing beneath the rhythm of our hearts.

The muse, the spark, the quiet whisper in the dark that turns longing into art.

The hand that lingers, the kiss that persists, the infinite unfolding of desire that fuels the dreamers and poets, creators and revolutionaries, and those who refuse to live without feeling.

Love is a collision of souls recognizing each other beyond time, the surrender of all logic for the sake of something too beautiful to measure.

This is a flame that does not burn, but illuminates.

A hunger that does not starve, but feeds.

A gravity that does not pull but sets free.

This book is a testament to love – her power, his depth, and of the ability to resurrect, to transform, to carve new worlds from the ruins of old ones within these realms.

May these words remind you that love is not meant to be contained.

Ethereal devotion is meant to be felt, to be lived, to be created again, in the way you move, how you dream, and in your capacity to love beyond reason.

Where galaxies kiss the Earth, love is not just a feeling – this force represents the entire universe.

About the Author

Jesse Jacoby is a dedicated father, expressionist, and advocate for compassion, equanimity, and purity. He expends energy adventuring in forests, creating, learning, playing, and writing.

Jesse is the founder and CEO of Soulspire: The Healing Playground (*soulspire.com*). This is a biohacking and purification center located near Lake Tahoe in Truckee, CA.

He is also the founder of the Global School of Purification (*schoolofpurity.com*), which is an educational course instructing how to regenerate health in the body.

Jesse is the author of The Raw Cure: Healing Beyond Medicine (1st & 2nd Editions), The Way Knows: Trusting Divine Orchestration, Gaia Speaks, Eating Plant-Based: The New Health Paradigm, Society's Anonymous, and My Quest to Conquer What Matters. His acoustic album, titled Light Night of the Soul, will be released in 2025.

Jesse@soulspire.com